DRIVEL

DELICIOUSLY BAD WRITING BY YOUR FAVORITE AUTHORS

EDITED BY
JULIA SCOTT

A Project of Litquake

A PERIGEE BOOK

A PERIGEE BOOK
Published by the Penguin Group
Penguin Group (USA) LLC
375 Hudson Street, New York, New York 10014

USA · Canada · UK · Ireland · Australia · New Zealand · India · South Africa · China

penguin.com

A Penguin Random House Company

Library of Congress Cataloging-in-Publication Data

Drivel : deliciously bad writing by your favorite authors / [edited by] Julia Scott.—First edition.
p.   cm.
ISBN 978-0-399-16888-8
1. American literature—21st century.   2. American wit and humor.   I. Scott, Julia.
PS536.3.D75   2014   2014013640
810.8'006—dc23

First edition: September 2014

PRINTED IN THE UNITED STATES OF AMERICA

10   9   8   7   6   5   4   3   2   1

Text design by Pauline Neuwirth

Most Perigee books are available at special quantity discounts for bulk purchases for sales
promotions, premiums, fund-raising, or educational use. Special books, or book excerpts, can
also be created to fit specific needs. For details, write: Special.Markets@us.penguingroup.com.

TERRIBLE CONTENTS

1
TOTALLY PROFESSIONAL

2
BAD ROMANCE

3
ILL-ADVISED CONFESSIONS

4
ODDITIES

5
DARK MATTER

6
TERRIBLE ANGST

PREFACE

The genesis for this project was a desperate idea for a fundraiser. Janis Cooke Newman and I were brainstorming some type of collaboration between San Francisco's Litquake literary festival and the Writers' Grotto collective, which might benefit Litquake.

Grotto writers reading from their work? "Who's going to pay to see that?" joked Janis, who of course is a member of the Grotto.

We continued racking our brains. It couldn't be just another reading or panel discussion. It needed some real zest. And then it suddenly hit me—what if we had these respected, professional writers read instead from the *worst* thing they'd ever written? The most shameful, embarrassing, precocious, clunky, sappy, immature, cloyingly earnest prose that somehow may have been stashed in a long-forgotten box.

Subconsciously, I think I was remembering a horrifically misguided paper I had written about hippies in the fourth grade. It was so ill-informed and painful that I could still recall some of the sentences verbatim. If I were ever to dig it up, it might amuse a roomful of people clutching cocktails. I would come off looking

---

Photos taken at Regreturature, *the annual live show that inspired this book.* © *Chris Hardy.*
From L to R: First row: *Ethel Rohan, Caroline Paul, David Duncan, Jeff Greenwald.*
Second row: *Isaac Fitzgerald, Katie Crouch, Stephen Elliott.*
Third row: *Heather Donahue, David Munro, Laura Fraser.*
Fourth row: *Todd Oppenheimer, Jack Boulware, Simon Rich, Mary Roach.*

pretty stupid, but perhaps other writers could be persuaded to also embarrass themselves for a worthy cause. (The "essay" is included here.)

But would it work? Would writers who ordinarily push themselves to be the best be willing to debase themselves and offer up a personal literary turd in the name of entertainment? This goes against everything writers strive for. It's hard enough to learn how to write well, to hustle working gigs, to get paid, to get published, to find readers, to make the world care about what you wrote. So why would anyone reverse the process and call attention to the fact their writing once sucked ass? And even more importantly, for our purposes, would they have saved any of it?

To everyone's surprise, from Janis and me to the authors, their friends, and the audience, the stage show titled *Regreturature* has become a hit. We've sold out all of our events over the past four years, and now you're holding this collection—*Drivel*—which includes several of the pieces we presented, plus many other gems.

It's always inspiring to hear great writing read aloud. But listening to a well-established author read from a cringeworthy teenage diary, or an earnest letter to President Nixon, or a groaner student poem is enlightening in a different way. It reminds all of us that writing takes work. That everybody does start somewhere, and often that somewhere is pretty crappy.

So in a sense, *Drivel* offers hope for all aspiring writers. And it also sends a warning. If you haven't thrown away your horrible writing, we may someday hunt you down and force you to share it onstage.

—Jack Boulware, cofounder of Litquake

INTRODUCTION

Right about now, you're probably feeling pretty good about yourself. You're holding a collection of shamefully bad writing by authors who have invested a lot of their careers in getting you to think they're pretty great. If you've ever aspired to greatness but were scared of sucking, or spent desperate hours pulling your hair out and throwing draft after draft in the trash, you recognize the cringing terror these authors are feeling right at this very moment. Have a care for them.

Why? Because there was a time, not so long ago, when their writing stank so badly it wouldn't even have been used to line a litter box. And yet the contributors in *Drivel: Deliciously Bad Writing by Your Favorite Authors* are doing the unthinkable: they are willing to impale themselves, in public, for your amusement.

In fact, the writing in this collection is so bad it deserves its own taxonomy of suckitude. There's abstruse and esoteric poetry (bad); incoherent and illogical short stories (worse); bumfuzzling proto-journalism (shameful); and pretentious, overwrought journal entries (just turn the page and we'll not speak of this again).

And all by your favorite bestselling authors. Yes, they've committed horrible crimes against the written word. But the lesson, if there is one, lies in what happened next.

They never stopped writing. And eventually, they began not to suck.

I conceived the idea for this book after performing at the second-annual live *Regreturature* show in San Francisco in 2012. I read from a journal entry I wrote as a twenty-year-old, gushing like a *Tiger Beat* teenybopper over an encounter with British playwright Tom Stoppard. ("It's enough to know that I am living IN THE SAME LIFETIME, let alone being in the same room!")

Who knew my earnest writerly crush on an eminent septuagenarian would supply so many laugh lines? I was delighted. But as the evening slipped by, I sensed a second feeling in the crowd: a sort of communal catharsis. Together, we'd transcended the pain and the humiliation of dredging up our stinkiest "work." And we'd turned it into a kind of public sacrifice.

By far the hardest part of putting this book together was getting authors to cough up their hoary hair balls. Some were seduced by the concept immediately and were forced to choose from a veritable catalog of tumescent masterworks.

Others not so much. No matter how I framed my plea, begging for some scrap of juvenilia or errant bit of mid-career offal—anything, really, that escaped the wrecking ball of good taste and discretion—a number of fellow writers were not swayed.

Their excuses were just a notch above "the dog ate my homework": "My mom threw out my early writing." "My boxes are buried in the attic." "I don't have anything that qualifies as bad enough to share." (A note on that last one: we don't believe you.)

Some writers expressed genuine regret, even as they confessed why they couldn't contribute. One bestselling novelist got straight to the point:

"My bad writing is so bad, and there's so much of it, and so little of the good, that it's just too painful to lay eyes on that stuff," he explained. (We understand.)

You're about to meet the dozens of contributors who volunteered to pluck their turgid treasures from the bottom of a locked and moldy vault. Thanks to these courageous but foolhardy writers, the world now knows the real meaning of a work in progress.

—Julia Scott, San Francisco Writers' Grotto

1

TOTALLY PROFESSIONAL

And why not guppies?
—Mary Roach

GUPPY LOVE

MARY ROACH

MARY ROACH is the author of the *New York Times* bestsellers *Stiff*, *Spook*, *Bonk*, *Packing for Mars*, and her latest, *Gulp: Adventures on the Alimentary Canal*. She was guest editor of *The Best American Science and Nature Writing 2011* and a winner of the American Association of Engineering Societies' Engineering Journalism Award, in a category for which, let's be honest, she was the sole entrant.

In my early twenties, I had a job in the public information office of the San Francisco SPCA. I was excited about this job, because for the first time in my limp, spotty almost-career I was being paid to write. One of the things I was occasionally tasked with writing was the "Pet Tips" column in the *San Francisco Examiner*. There was no byline on this column because there was no columnist. The writer changed from week to week, depending on who had managed to weasel out of it, who had pretended to be under the gun with, say, a press release on Holiday Dangers for Pets ("Deck the halls with caution this Christmas . . ."). I was dismayed by the absence of a byline because I thought I might one day use some of my "Pet Tips" columns as writing samples. Not all of them, mind you. Just the really good ones. And without a byline, how could an editor be sure I hadn't just clipped someone else's wry, sparkling guppy piece from the paper and claimed it as my own?

I seem to recall being proud of the phrase "minute fry" and the sly humor of baby guppies emerging "individually wrapped" in clear membranes. Obviously the word "plastic" to describe the clear membranes is a mistake, the sort of airheaded gaffe that still from time to time shows up in my books. My long-standing inability to wrap things up smoothly (with or without clear plastic) is also in evidence here, in the jarring, graceless shift from oxygen concentrations to "So let's hear it for guppies!"

—M.R.

Pet tips

Guppy love

AND WHY NOT guppies? All too often bought as food for other fish, the common (non-fancy) guppy is a likable, hardy, easy-to-care-for pet. Their demands are few: a box of guppy food and an aquarium full of water. (They should be fed twice a day and the water temperature shouldn't drop below 60 degrees.)

As pets go, guppies are an unbeatable educational tool. Remember the Visible Man — that nifty GI-Joe-sized fellow made of clear plastic so kids could look inside and see his organs? Well, guppies are kind of like that. You can look into a female's belly and see minute fry (baby guppies) moving about.

The fact that the female's eggs are fertilized and allowed to develop inside her makes the guppy a rarity among fish. Many fish lay their eggs someplace to be fertilized later by the male. (Internal fertilization also means that guppies are one of the few fish that afford a glimpse into the fascinating world of piscine mating practices.)

After a month's gestation, the spectacle of guppy birth begins. If you're lucky enough to be watching at the time, you'll get to see 50 or so fry being expelled into the water, individually wrapped in clear plastic membranes. Within seconds, the guppies break out and swim away.

At this point, another fascinating, if somewhat less heartwarming phenomenon takes place. Since guppies breed so often and produce such large batches of fry, nature has devised an interesting way of keeping the guppy population explosion under control: Once their fry have hatched, the male and female begin feeding on some of their young. Try not to let it bother you. It's a natural part of the guppy way of life, and enough fry survive to keep the population thriving. You can separate the babies in another tank, but in several months time you'll have to separate the babies of the next generation, and so on. It may be best to think of it as nature's own birth control and let things take their course.

Guppies also have another form of natural birth control. As time goes on and the tank gets crowded, the females will begin having fewer babies. It's a hormonal response to environmental changes, such as lower concentrations of oxygen in the water.

So let's hear it for guppies. They may not be as cuddly as puppies, but they are an amazing little species of fish.

DEAR BUTTHOLE

JAMES NESTOR has written for *Outside* magazine, *Men's Journal, Dwell*, the *New York Times, San Francisco Magazine, Salon*, the *San Francisco Chronicle*, and numerous other publications. His first nonfiction book, *Deep: Freediving, Renegade Science, and What the Ocean Tells Us About Ourselves*, was published in June 2014. His long-form piece *Half-Safe*, about the only around-the-world journey by land and sea in the same vehicle ever attempted (and completed), was published by the *Atavist* in 2013. Nestor owns a 1977 Mercedes that runs on used cooking oil and a 1979 Sebring-Vanguard electric CitiCar, both of which are for sale. He lives in San Francisco.

//

The best thing about graduating with a bachelor's degree in literature from a crappy college in the 1990s is that I never had to worry about getting a real job. There weren't any. No employer cared that I could argue the difference between Post-Colonialism and New Historicism, or recite the first four stanzas of *Song of Myself*, or knew that George Eliot was a woman—nor should they. Employers wanted someone with real-world skills, or, at minimum, someone who had the ability to write and think clearly. Literature courses teach you neither.

While full-time jobs were elusive, there were plenty of menial, temporary jobs: stuffing mailboxes, data entry, consulting new mothers on diapering products, delivering chicken, estimating the flat paper dimensions of a folded envelope. These were all jobs I held a year after graduating.

The least degrading of the lot was a two-week gig filling in for a vacationing secretary at a hotel management company. My boss, a red-faced lawyer named Jim (who I later learned got his bachelor's in sociology), took a liking to me, or took pity on me, or both. After my two weeks were up, Jim kept me on as a junior copywriter. I was eventually hired full-time.

What does a junior copywriter at a hotel management company do? Not much, I soon discovered. I spent my days nibbling on leftover Entenmann's coffee cake in the kitchen, reading every line of every *New Yorker* every week, and grabbing frozen yogurt with the hotel management's advertising department, who, I found, didn't work much either.

I also starting fiddling with this thing called the Internet, where I discovered something called electronic mail. And that's where this story begins.

—J.N.

The Kimpton Group offices were antiquated, even by 1990s standards, and only a select few of us had Internet access on our computers. Lisa, the company art director who sat in the cubicle next to me, had the Internet and she also had email. A few days after I started, she showed me how to use it. When Lisa would go to lunch, I'd hop in her chair, plug in her password, log on, and write to my friends. Soon my friends were writing back. By week's end, Lisa and I were sharing her Kimpton Group email address.

A few days later, our shared address received a lewd and crudely written email directed to me. It was from my brother, John. He was organizing a bachelor party and was inquiring as to whether I, or the other fifteen friends on the group email, was going. His note read, simply:

```
Hey Dicks:

Vegas. May 10-12. Don't be a pussy.

John
```

I waited for Lisa to go to lunch then sat down at her computer, logged in, and responded to John's email in equally profane language. When I was done, I scrolled up to the recipient box and typed in the word "all," intending to reply all to my brother and our friends.

What I didn't realize is that I had forgotten to put the word "reply" before "all." This meant my lewd response didn't go to my brother and our friends; instead, it went to all—literally, all, as in *everyone* in Lisa's address book.

All 502 people.

. . . to Lisa's parents, her grandparents, her boyfriend, his parents, to Kimpton Group's national sales staff, to Kimpton's *clients*, to *their* clients. To the president of the Make-A-Wish Foundation.

And there was no sign that the vulgar message I had written was sent from me. It contained only Lisa's email address, and her signature.

A few minutes later, when the first of the 502 contacts opened their inboxes and clicked on the email sent from Lisa Cowen, Art Director at the Kimpton Group—this is the message that greeted them:

```
Dear Butthole:

Listen, this job doesn't pay me enough to buy
shaving cream. Perhaps I can whore myself and
work up the scratch to make the party. I'll try
that tonight and let you know.

Fuck You
```

That's the message that awaited Lisa's boss, Kimpton Group's sixty-one-year-old conservative Republican president, when he got back from lunch.

Unaware of what I had done, I logged off the computer, grabbed my bag, went to a doctor's appointment, then went home.

Meanwhile, Lisa's inbox exploded with responses. One of the first people to respond to her—or rather, my—nasty note was her childhood priest. He wrote:

```
Lisa:

Are you OK?—Please call me.—I'm very worried.
```

There were angry and confused messages from the vice president of sales, from the regional managers and hotel union representatives. They all thought this was Lisa's coup d'état—that she was quitting, and sending out a final farewell fuck-you to the world.

There were voicemails too, from parents and concerned relatives. Lisa's grandmother was particularly distraught at being addressed as a butthole.

Lisa returned from lunch and quickly figured out what had happened, what I had done. She sprinted around the office and tried to delete the email from as many empty computers as she could. To the rest of the recipients, she sent an apology, explaining that there had been a mix-up. For many, however, her apologetic note just made her seem even more insane. The damage had been done.

I got home that night and noticed there was a message on my answering machine. It was Lisa. She was short of breath, half crying, half laughing, all chokes and chuckles and sobs.

"NESTOR!" she cried. "You are so fucking dead." Then she explained the situation. I suddenly realized that within two months, I had sabotaged the first real job I had ever had in my life.

I returned to the Kimpton Group office the next day and prepared to pack up my stuff and hit the streets. Lisa showed up a little later.

"You know, you're an idiot," she said, walking over to my side of the cubicle. "I know," I said. She told me that although she was tempted, she didn't rat me out. Nobody knew the email came from me. She took the hit and so I was safe.

I handed her a 40-ouncer of Olde English in a brown paper bag that I had picked up on the way to work, trying to make light of the awful situation.

Lisa exhaled, grabbed the 40, and said, "Don't you ever mention this again." Then she turned around, walked back to her computer, logged on to her email, and changed the password.

TAKE A CHANCE ON ME

NEAL POLLACK

NEAL POLLACK is the author of eight books of fiction and nonfiction, including the bestselling parenting memoir *Alternadad*, the cult satirical classic *The Neal Pollack Anthology of American Literature*, and the novels *Jewball*, *Downward-Facing Death*, and *Open Your Heart*. He has contributed to eight million magazines, newspapers, and websites. A flat-track roller derby announcer, certified yoga instructor, graduate of the Jaguar High-Performance Driving Academy, and three-time *Jeopardy!* champion, Pollack lives in Austin, Texas, with his wife and son.

///

When I was fresh out of journalism school, I was actually a pretty good writer, or at least a competent one. Maybe there were some diary entries here and there that would make the future me blush. I seem to remember one from 1990 where I wrote, "I am becoming increasingly influenced by the comedic stylings of *Saturday Night Live*." But for the most part, my J-school background bled me of artistic pretension. For years, I wrote nothing worse than boring summaries of district water-board hearings.

I reserved my stupidest, purplest prose for my job applications. In those days, I believed that no career height was beyond my achievement. Even though I had, at best, an average collection of clips, I continually applied to

Rolling Stone, and *Esquire*, and *Spy*, and *GQ*, and *Vanity Fair*, and any other magazine that I could find at the barbershop. I oversang my praises and sent them stupid little humor pieces. I humiliated myself, even if I was the only one who ever read the letters.

Below, you'll find two egregious examples, which I wrote in 1992. The originals no longer exist because I sent them away and because the computer I wrote them on is slowly decaying in a landfill somewhere. Let them be a warning to young careerists everywhere: this is what you sound like.

—N.P.

In 1992, I wrote a "job application" letter to Tina Brown, who was the editor of the *New Yorker* at the time.

Dear Ms. Brown,

I'll cut to the quick. I would like to work for the *New Yorker*. And I imagine with the big change-over, you may need lots of editorial help. So I'm throwing my hat into the ring, and asking you to consider hiring me as an editorial assistant for your new project.

I've been precociously reading the *New Yorker* for some time now. And I am a devotee of the current magazine, as well as of its historical heritage. Most of the writers I respect most, living and dead, have written for your magazine at some time. I'm willing to cut my journalistic and literary teeth elsewhere, if I can't get a job at the *New Yorker*, but I'm determined not to end up anywhere else.

The resume I've enclosed doesn't indicate this, but I've been working as a freelance writer since graduating two months ago. I've been doing pretty well, but I'm still waiting for the big score. Maybe you could help. I strongly encourage you to take a chance on me, but if I don't suit your needs at this time, thank you for reviewing my application. I look forward to hearing from you.

I also wrote a letter to Strobe Talbott, who was at the time an editor at *Time* magazine and later became a deputy secretary of state under Bill Clinton. He was starting a new magazine that I don't believe ever happened.

Dear Mr. Talbott,

I'm a damn good editor. I'm young and gutsy, as a marine in combat. My terse, tough prose style would make Raymond Chandler weep. Somewhere, somehow, the grapevine told me that you're starting a magazine called *Globe Review*. Said vine also let me know that the staff will be small, which means you're not hiring too many people. Being the low man on the totem pole is fine with me.

Your magazine sounds original, smart, and progressive, sophisticated but not shallow. Of course, I'm just guessing. Can you go global without me? I think so. Should you? I think not. Or at least I hope not. I'll do good work as an assistant editor, copy editor, or researcher. I'll be in New York City from November 11 through 17. If you'd like to interview me, you can contact me at the Chicago address on my resume until then. Thank you for reviewing my application. And I look forward to seeing the magazine, whether I am part of it or not.

PROFESSOR EATANOFF
(AND HIS GUIDEBOOK OF PROPER PROCEDURE FOR FLESHEATERS)

DANIEL CLOWES is the acclaimed cartoonist of the seminal comic book series *Eightball*, and the graphic novels *Ghost World*, *David Boring*, *Ice Haven*, *Wilson*, *Mister Wonderful,* and *The Death-Ray*, as well as the subject of the monograph *The Art of Daniel Clowes: Modern Cartoonist*, published in conjunction with a major retrospective at the Oakland Museum of California. He is an Oscar-nominated screenwriter; the recipient of numerous awards, including the PEN Award for literature, Eisner, Harvey, and Ignatz; and a frequent cover artist for the *New Yorker*. He is married and lives in Oakland, California.

I wish I could just write this off as mere juvenilia, but I was actually twenty-three years old when I created this tasteful gem, a year shy of my first professional work. I did this strip, along with several others of equal merit (*Doctor Motherfucker, I Married a Human Worm*) with the intent of selling them to *National Lampoon* magazine, or possibly even the *New Yorker* (!), imagining in my youthful delusion that America was secretly clamoring for passive-aggressive adolescent cannibal humor. I actually put this page in my illustration portfolio, which would probably explain why I never got a single assignment.

—D.C.

CLICK HERE!
WHAT I DID FOR MONEY

DAVID MUNRO is an award-winning filmmaker based in San Francisco. His latest project is *Stand Up Planet*, a documentary about young, outspoken international comedians sparking social change through humor. Munro's first feature, *Full Grown Men*, won the 2007 Sundance Channel Undiscovered Gems Award. Prior to filmmaking, Munro wrote shamefully lucrative advertisements.

The mid-nineties were a heady time for me. That's when I fell in love with filmmaking and at the same time fell out of love with my career that up to that point had paid me very well, which was to write advertisements. So I quit my day job and entered film school. I had become so militantly disillusioned with consumer culture as part of my transformation that I actually wrote in my film school application that ads were "pornography." Which is not only ironic, but, as you'll see very shortly, prophetic.

It was around the time that I started making my first short film that I realized that making movies is hella expensive. At the time, I was working split shifts as a cabdriver and a hotel desk clerk. I got a call from a friend offering me a freelance copywriting job. He said this job would pay me $1,000 a day. Of course, my mind exploded with all the gaffer's tape and film stock that I could buy for $1,000 a day. Here's how he pitched me the job:

"Bro, I've got good news and better news. The good news is, this job is going to pay us a shit-ton of money. The better news is, it's for a porn site."

This was a dilemma. But I was desperate. The client was GameLink.com, and they were the world's first online porn superstore.

Without further ado, here are the interactive web banners that I wrote for the Walmart of sleaze.

—D.M.

AD #1

Very classy. My apologies if you're a lefty.

AD #2

The film that this paid for went to Sundance, by the way.

AD #3

AD #4

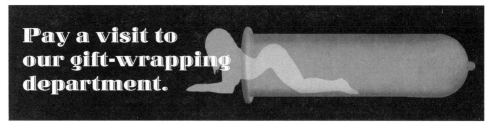

Some of these were better than others.

AD #5

That one didn't run. Even they passed on that one.

And finally, this is the only one I'm proud of:

AD #6

D.A.R.E. TO SAY "NO" TO MARIJUANA

MARIE C. BACA

MARIE C. BACA is a San Francisco Bay Area–based writer. Her nonfiction is primarily about people on the fringes of society: morgue workers, day laborers, Bigfoot hunters, cockfighting enthusiasts, UFO trackers, and the wrongfully convicted. She's investigated the proliferation of toxic waste sites in poor communities and the effects of fracking on rural populations. Recently, she's begun writing humor, personal essays, and fiction. Her work has appeared in the *Wall Street Journal*, *San Francisco Chronicle*, *ProPublica*, *McSweeney's Internet Tendency*, and *Salon*, among other publications. Baca holds a bachelor's degree in human biology and a master's degree in journalism from Stanford University. Visit her at MarieCBaca.com.

Baca with a rat on her head.

If, like me, you went to an American public school in the '80s and '90s, you probably encountered the Drug Abuse Resistance Education (D.A.R.E.) program, which taught students how to "just say 'NO'" to drugs. While the program's goals may have been admirable, the execution was often ludicrous: in my elementary school in San Diego, for example, reading time was often cut short to learn about Schedule III narcotics (we were ten). I guess it's no surprise then that I won the fifth-grade D.A.R.E. skit-writing competition with a piece that made *Reefer Madness* look like Shakespeare.

Fortunately, this literary gem was performed in front of the entire school.

Unfortunately, we were not allowed to use props that looked like real drugs, nor did we know what real drugs looked like. So we pretended to smoke rolls of gift wrap and hoped for the best. I'd like to apologize to my classmates for the misinformation we presented that day, although I will say that if you smoke a three-foot joint, hallucinations of twins will be the least of your problems.

—M.B.

[MARIE and JULIA stand next to each other looking bored. Suddenly, JULIA notices the two gift wrap tube "joints" in front of her.]

JULIA: Hey, look what I found!

MARIE: What is that?

JULIA: It's marijuana or weed. If you smoke it, you will relax.

MARIE: Is it illegal?

JULIA: Yes.

MARIE: I don't want to get in trouble.

JULIA: Come on, don't be a loser! You loser! Just smoke it!

MARIE: I don't know . . .

[Enter the MYSTERIOUS TWINS, holding a sign that says "POOF" as well as a giant remote control. Everything they say is in unison, because they are twins. Also, they are dressed the same.]

MYSTERIOUS TWINS: Poof!

JULIA: Who are you?

MYSTERIOUS TWINS: We are the two Mysterious Twins! We've come here to show you what will happen in the future if you do drugs. Fast-forward! *[They click the giant remote.]*

[JULIA and MARIE spin around wildly to indicate the passage of time.]

MYSTERIOUS TWINS: *[Hold up sign that says "The Future."]* This is the future!

[JULIA and MARIE pick up the joints and "smoke" them.]

MARIE: Whoa.

JULIA: This is a good blunt.

MARIE: I am stoned.

MYSTERIOUS TWINS: Marijuana is a very dangerous drug! It can cause short-term memory loss and anxiety and is very addictive!

JULIA: I don't feel good.

[JULIA and MARIE begin coughing. They fall to the ground dramatically. They are dead.]

MYSTERIOUS TWINS: *[They press the giant remote.]* Rewind!

[JULIA and MARIE get up and spin around wildly again.]

MYSTERIOUS TWINS: *[Hold up sign that says "Today."]* It is today, again.

JULIA: Wow, thanks Mysterious Twins!

MARIE: Thanks for showing us the future!

JULIA: Yeah, now we know about the dangers of drugs.

MARIE: I don't want to die.

JULIA: Let's just say "no" to marijuana.

MARIE: Okay!

FIN

TRENDING NOW

CHARLES YU is the author of three books, including some that have actually been liked by people, unlike the piece he contributed to *Drivel*, which is apparently impossible for anyone to like. He regrets a lot of things he has said and done, but despite the title of this collection, he doesn't necessarily regret having written a bad thing, or lots of bad things. It's just part of writing, you know? Everyone has bad stuff. Except Karen Russell. She's a robot. A fiction-writing robot genius. Someone get her.

L ooking at this again almost gave me a seizure. I'm not sure what I was thinking, but apparently I was in some state of fractured, hyperstimulated consciousness where I was incapable of writing a sentence longer than four or five words. That'd be bad enough as an experience for a reader, but the truth is I actually wrote this for a reading series, to be performed by an actor onstage. I was unofficially commissioned to write it, and I did, and I sent it in, and then I never heard back. Literally, not one word. I'm not sure how it's possible, but I think the reading series may have actually ended because my submission was so bad. As with almost anything, it's not absolutely or irretrievably bad all the way down to a molecular level. I mean, if you squint hard, and are in the right frame of mind (that is, you have had more than six cans of Red

Bull), you can imagine a time and place and state of inebriation in which this could, with much more work, precision, nuance, and wit, have turned into something halfway decent. Or maybe you can't.

And it gets a little worse—I was thirty-six when I wrote this. Not sixteen, or twenty-six. In the grand scale of my life, I basically wrote this yesterday. If you think, when you get past a certain point, that you can never write something truly abysmal, well, this piece right here suggests otherwise.

—C.Y.

I'm a good person. Or at least not a bad person. Pretty good. Almost good. Ninetieth percentile. That sounds too high. Eightieth percentile. Top quintile, is that what it's called? Good enough. I care about other people. I care about caring about other people. No I don't. No, wait, I do. I care. Is caring enough? It's a start. But I have to do more. I have to do something. What should I care about? I don't know. I don't know what to care about. I have to learn more to know what to care about. I have to do something now. Something real, something big, start today, this moment, change myself, change the world a little bit, just a little bit, engage with the world. I have to go:

To the Internet.

I'm opening a browser window. A window to the world. The news. What is happening? Wars. There are wars going on. There are people dying of curable diseases. Insert real stats here. That's a note to myself, to learn stats later. This would be more impactful if I had real stats. God I hate that word. Impactful. That's not even a word. Is it? I should look it up. Note to self: look that up later.

I don't even want to know if it's a real word. If it is, it still sucks. If someone says impactful, I automatically don't like that person. That word gives me goose bumps, the bad kind. That word makes me flinch. It makes me wince. Wincing and flinching at the same time. Winching. That's a word. Impactful, on the other hand: still not a word. It's, I don't know what it is. A non-word. A damaged fragment of language. An orphan. A mangled idea turned into a sound, a sound which sounds like a word, but it's really just a noise. I'm off track here. Stats. Here we go, let's see. A portal. My window is into a portal. A news portal. A hole. I'm looking through a hole at the world. I can point my hole and see what I want to see. Blank people die of blank horrible disease every year. Oh my God that's depressing. Ugh, I need stats. It would be so much more powerful with stats. I'm a good person, or at least I want to be a good person, and a good person would know stats. A good person would do something about this. I should volunteer. How do I do that? Click on this link, oh man I love the Internet and

HELLO

—Hello?

HELLO

—Who are you?

I'M THE INTERNET. HERE IS WHAT IS TRENDING NOW

—I don't want to know what is trending now. I want the news.

TRENDING NOW. NOW. WHAT'S MORE NEWSWORTHY THAN THAT?

—I need to know what to care about.

TRENDING NOW:

—I don't care about that.

HERE ARE THE TOP FIVE KARDASHIANS

—I told you, I don't care about that. And Kourtney is obviously the best Kardashian.

HERE ARE THE TOP FIVE TELEVISON SHOWS: YOGA WITH THE STARS. YODELING WITH THE STARS. EATING YOGURT WITH THE STARS

—That's not interesting to me. What is interesting to me is, well, I'm not exactly sure what's interesting to me but whatever it turns out to be, one thing I am sure of, really sure of is, oh my God is that a baby panda hugging a baby koala? No, no, stop it. I'm a good person. Eightieth percentile. Certainly no lower than seventy-fifth. Top quartile. I am going to volunteer. If my schedule permits. If not, then I'll donate. That's perfect. I work, to make the money, and then I send it to people that need the money, in a faraway place that I know about from commercials. It's how much? Oh I'm good for that. Put me down for, wait that's every month? Okay maybe, huh, hmmm, hrrrmmm, okay donate is on my list, I will donate, maybe a little later, I don't even have my credit card with me, where is my wallet? Oh crap, it's all the way on the other side of the room. Okay donate later, but what can I do now? Right now? Anything that doesn't require a credit card. I can sign a petition. Click yes on that box. But, ugh, that takes me to a link and that seems like a lot of text to read. I have to scroll down, all the way to the bottom? And then, give my address. Hmm, why do they need that? Okay, well, maybe I don't sign that petition yet, but at least I know about it. I don't know the positions of the left and the right on the issue and what the science says but I do know the issue exists. That's something. That's more than most people can say. That makes me, at least, I don't know, sixtieth percentile? Maybe that's a little aggressive. The median. Smack dab in the middle. That's not bad. By definition, it's not bad. It's not good, but well, I can work on it. Starting now. Or now. What's going on now?

HERE IS WHAT IS TRENDING NOW:
KENNY G DIVORCE
CHUCK NORRIS
AUSTRALIAN SHARK ATTACK
IS AFRICA A COUNTRY?
BANKRUPTCY PROTECTION
TRAMPOLINING WITH THE STARS
YO-YOING WITH THE STARS, STARRING YO-YO MA

—Why am I so unhappy?

—Why do I keep doing this again and again?

—Why am I with him?

—Why is she with me?

—Why aren't things turning out the way I thought they would?

—What do I look at now? What is trending now? No, shut up. How do I clear my head? How can I think straight? How can I even think about what I want to think about? What can I do, what do I do?

What am I supposed to do now? And now? And now? And now? What do I do now?

SIMON RICH

SIMON'S NEWS PAGE

SIMON RICH has written for the *New Yorker*, the *Believer*, and *McSweeney's*. His books have been published in a dozen languages. His latest collection is called *Spoiled Brats*.

These days, I write joke books and gags for the movies. There was a time, though, when I wanted to be taken seriously as a writer. That's why, when I was five, I founded a hard-hitting, muckraking newspaper. The year was 1989 and the world was changing fast. The Berlin Wall was coming down, Nelson Mandela was making waves, and Mr. Brockman was introducing shapes and colors at my kindergarten. I was reporting from the front lines of history.

Simon's News Page was critically acclaimed by everyone (Mom, Dad). Somehow, though, we folded after just five issues. A few factors contributed to our demise. As an investigative journalist, my scope was limited by the fact that I wasn't allowed to leave the apartment. Low circulation was another problem. I was so desperate to increase our readership, I resorted to printing sensationalist headlines ("Bubble Gum," "Rock and Roll"). In hindsight, this was the beginning of the end.

The biggest blow to *Simon's News Page* occurred when my mother, whom I dictated the newspaper to, informed me that she no longer had time to type up my articles whenever I wanted her to. When you lose your publisher, it's hard to recover. Still, I'm proud of the work we did. I feel like we told it straight, changed some minds, and made a real difference in apartment 6A.

Below are some excerpts from *Simon's News Page*.

—S.R.

NEWS

[NOTE: I have a brother Nathaniel, he's four years older than me. I was very much on the Nathaniel "beat."]

BUBBLE GUM

Nathaniel Rich blew a bubble that was almost as big as my face. I thought it was pretty good. It was the biggest bubble I ever saw. It was almost as big as the S on Superman's chest—I mean bigger. So that's all for the top story today.

ROCK AND ROLL

Nathaniel likes rock and roll. He even watches MTV. He loves rock and roll so much that he even talks about it. In fact he doesn't like it, he LOVES it. He likes it even more than baseball cards. That's it.

ADVERTISEMENTS

Here is a list of what you could get your child for Christmas.

1. G.I. Joe Figures.
2. Police Academy.

3. Double Dare.
4. Ring Raiders.
5. Some Clothes.

REVIEWS

[NOTE: This is a review of the classic Tim Burton *Batman* movie. My review was hindered by the fact that my mother did not let me see the film, due to scariness, even though my older brother had been allowed to see it.]

I am telling you that "Batman" isn't good at all. There might be a movie about it but that doesn't have anything to do with going Batman crazy! A month passed and everyone is still Batman crazy. Why not tell the actors and everything that Batman isn't so great? . . . We are real and Batman isn't.

EDITORIALS

MIKHAIL GORBACHEV

Mikhail Gorbachev is a pretty good leader of France. He makes peace in the entire world.

MR. BROCKMAN IS NICE

Mr. Brockman is so nice, he even has good projects like journals. We write in the journals every time it is time for journals. I love the journals the most. I always like doing the journals. I hope I get to do the journals forever.

LETTER TO THE NOSE

JOSH McHUGH is the CEO of Attention Span Media, a digital agency with clients in the entertainment and hospitality industries. Before joining Attention Span in 2008, he was a contributing editor at *Wired* magazine, an associate editor at *Forbes*, and a writer for *Vanity Fair*, *Outside*, and other publications. McHugh graduated from Yale in 1992 with a bachelor's degree in English. His efforts to dunk a basketball are the subject of *Dunkumentary*, a short documentary that screened at the Cannes Film Festival in 2009.

The first piece of mine that was published in a non-school-sanctioned publication was never meant to be published at all. It was 1992, my first year out of college. While perusing one of Philadelphia's more eclectic newsstands, I lucked into a copy of *The Nose*. This was during the heyday of *Spy Magazine*, which I read regularly. But I always came away from *Spy* feeling like I'd shared an elevator with James Spader's character Steff from *Pretty in Pink*.

Nose, on the other hand, had all the gonzo funny of *Spy* without the jaded Upper East Side snottiness. This was the kind of magazine I could see myself working for.

This is my attempt to get a job at the magazine. I sat down at the IBM Selectric that I had bought for $1 at a yard sale. Its motor was ill-calibrated, which made the machine jumpy, causing the lines of text to look as though they'd been hiccupped onto the page. It also had a hyperactive *Z* key that deployed at random. Propping my *Nose* issue on the basement worktable next to the Selectric, I launched into a job application letter that, in retrospect, was a blend of thinly veiled arrogance, desperation, and atrocious spelling.

I sent the letter off to *The Nose*'s San Francisco headquarters and, not that surprisingly, didn't hear back. The letter did get their attention, however. A few months later, back at school for a tailgate party, a friend told me that my piece in *The Nose* was the funniest thing he'd read in a long time.

"What piece in *The Nose*?"

"You know, that thing where you were pretending to be looking for a job?"

I hunted the magazine down and finally saw the response, which was:

"We have no job for you, Joshua. But, when you pitch yourself to a magazine for employment, here's a tip: proof for typos. Yale, eh?"

—J.M.

The Mail

LAST YEAR, while I was still in college, i [sic] bought a copy of your magazine. It was the issue with the Bettie Page doppelgangers on the cover and in the middle. I really was amused by the article about the foot/shoe slave network; the article ended with a great pun, about "sexual fayvas." I was very impressed with the article on the funeral home industry—those bastards. I sat down and wrote for an hour on how I want things done when I go; your article has, at least in my case, or rather will cost the funeral homes of the nation thousands of dollars.

None of those frills for me; it will be, per William Carlos Williams' specs, "a rough dray to drag over the ground." The only frivolous expense will be the substitution of Tanqueray for the Clyde's gin which was my mainstay during the difficult/living years. Both of the last statements are a sort of segue into the coming statement that I was an English major while at Yale. Now that I have graduated, I spend a large portion of my waking hours down here in the basement of my mother's house, typing letters of disapproval to my college friends who have taken jobs counting beans for the man in various New York skyscrapers; other times I drive nails and carry wood for my uncle who is a contractor, though sensitive to the bitter ironies, in New Jersey; this way I can write and put the nachos bell-grande on they [sic] tray as well.

Overall, your magazine is quite funny, [but] without being bitterly smug/smugly bitter like *Spy* magazine. I have been making fun of people sinece [sic] I was a little kid, but I generally eschew the sneering approach. It seems that you at *The Nose* do, too.

More than enough about me: 5'9" 164 lbs., hair: black; nails: well-chewwed [sic], major in cllege [sic]: English w/concentration in poetry or Poetry; musical preference: smart, anti-karaoke in general; 5 o'clock shadow: permanent; travel plans: Australia in April '93 thru Sept. '93; will work for food, housing, minor luxury items, aspirin; I would like to work for your magazine in some capacity. If you can't pay me hardly anything, I could probably get a job in San Fran as a sandwich-board guy or a peyote button. Get back to me soon.

Joshua McHugh
Pottstown, PA

We have no job for you, Joshua, but when you pitch yourself to magazines for employment, here's a tip: proof for typos. Yale, eh?

2

BAD ROMANCE

"Do you play piano?"
she asked, looking at his
hands.
"No," he said, still
smiling. "Only
avocados."

—Ellen Sussman

OUT OF THE MOUTHS OF VIRGINS

ETHEL ROHAN

ETHEL ROHAN was born and raised in Dublin and now lives in San Francisco. She is the author of two story collections, *Goodnight Nobody* and *Cut Through the Bone*. She would hate you to think she has *ever* vomited in a car. Visit her at EthelRohan.com.

Fierce is how I imagined myself as I wrote "Out of the Mouths of Virgins"—attempting a kind of subversive erotic writing that would speak to the largely silenced sexcapades of my fellow Irishwomen. At nineteen, sexually active, and in love for the first time (or so I imagined), my body hummed with needs my church, culture, and parents insisted were sins. When I couldn't find enough horny girls like me in stories—getting it on, and often getting it wrong—I was determined to become the Irish author to write the raw and real sexual tales of my contemporaries into the canon. Where were our voices among the sad and stale tales of wives lying under heaving husbands, eyes squeezed shut?

My own complex and troubled relationship with sex affected this story, which is hardly a harlequin romance. Vomit rarely figures in erotic literature, for instance. The results were a little *too* real.

—E.R.

Inside the dim, smoky pub, Molly's vagina throbbed. *Tirlee*, her mother had called the body part. Girls had tirlees and boys had willies. Jaysus. Why was she thinking tirlees and willies? She wasn't a girl anymore. She was seventeen and about to be deflowered. A flash of herself ripping white petals from a daisy crossed her mind and she threw up her imagined pale arm and tossed the soft, severed pieces into the air like confetti.

She looked at Barry standing at the bar, so tall and broad and his eyes as black as his hair, and her vagina started up again like a thumping heartbeat. She loved Barry and she was going to give herself to him tonight. Fully. She recalled the shower of daisy petals she'd imagined raining down on her just minutes earlier and believed she and Barry would marry some day, a warm feeling spreading over her like hot water on a teabag.

Barry parked his Da's blue Renault at their usual spot in the Phoenix Park, right next to the polo fields. They'd been going out together since New Year's Eve (three months, two days, and twenty-two-and-a-half hours to be exact) and had probably made out in this very spot some fifty times. Always, she stopped Barry and wouldn't let him go all the way, just let him hump her with most of their clothes still on. But not tonight. Tonight they would get gloriously, biblically naked and he would enter her, fill her, complete her. She looked at him, trying to appear a seductress. He looked back at her, blinking hard, like he was trying to keep her in focus. God, they were both drunk. So drunk.

"Tonight's the night," she said, trying to sound her sexiest.

His head snapped back, as if she'd slapped him. "It is?"

She nodded, her teeth biting into her lower lip like she'd seen in films. All their other dates, she'd worn her ugliest knickers to steadfast her resolve to wait, but tonight she wore black lacy thongs. Just seeing her inside those, Barry might well spill himself.

He lowered the driver's seat and pulled her onto him. She tried not to look at his red, damp face or listen to his aroused sounds, more like bleating than moans. Tried not to think that he reminded her of that orangutan at the zoo last summer descending on an enormous mound of bananas, his teeth bared, lips curled inside out, and falling over his own limbs with excitement. She squeezed her eyes shut and let Barry remove her bra and then her best knickers. His head dipped to her hard nipple and his lips latched on. He made suckling baby sounds.

She slapped the side of his head. "You never even noticed me knickers?"

"What about your knickers?" he asked.

"They're new, sexy."

"Yeah, all right, nice." His lips wrapped around her nipple again.

Again she slapped his head. "I paid big money for them knickers. They're fancy."

"Fine, your knickers are fancy, gorgeous. Now can we get on with it."

He angled on the driver's seat and maneuvered her body so that she was lying on her back and he was straddling her. He slipped one, two, three fingers inside her. She was wet, so wet, and alive, so alive—a slick, throbbing organ between her legs. Like she'd just given birth to her own heart. It wouldn't hurt, she reassured herself. There would be no blood. Only her juices and his juices and their love, all spilling out, oozing.

He pulled her hand to his penis and they both stroked it.

"I've got it," she said, proud, confident, and he let her take over, her solo of solos. His face puffed and turned purple and he made grunting, wounded noises. "Stop," he said. "Let's make this last."

He repositioned them both on the seat so he was now lying on his back and she was lying on top. He pushed her head down his body and her insides grinned, knowing what he wanted, knowing what she was going to give him at last. She grabbed his penis, its purple-red top like a bruised eye, and took him into her mouth, hoped she was doing it right. He moaned and his hand pressed the back of her head. She thought her eyes were going to pop out of her face. Then, no, oh no, her stomach retched and she vomited all over him.

"I'm sorry," she said, her hand at her mouth.

Barry cleaned himself off and wanted back to business. His mouth worked her neck and then he kissed her again, even after she'd puked up vodka and Diet Coke and burger and chips. Next, he was humping her for real. They were naked and he was inside her and pushing at her like he wanted to go right through her. This is love, she told herself. This is my first time. I'm never going to forget my first time. Never going to forget Barry. She tried to settle in, to quicken her breathing, to feel aroused again, to have her vagina throb like a heart again, but something wasn't working. The horses! she thought. The horses that raced around the polo fields out there right next to the car after a little white ball. She tried to imagine the rhythm and race of the horses, the thud of their hooves in the dirt. She pictured the magnificent animals, their sleek coats and rippling muscles, their strong legs. Giddy up, she thought, giddy up. She moved her body and made her noises in time to the horses' gallop. She was close to climax. Her toes were curling. Barry jerked away from her, his teeth clenched and his penis in both hands. He sprayed her with his juices and she thought of a sparkler going off. He collapsed on top of her, panting.

"That was fucking great," he said.

She looked past him and into the blackness dazzled with stars. Molly and Barry, she thought. Tirlees and willies, she thought. She thought, all the things that rhyme.

THE AFFAIR

ELLEN SUSSMAN

ELLEN SUSSMAN is the national best-selling author of four novels, *A Wedding in Provence*, *The Paradise Guest House*, *French Lessons*, and *On a Night Like This*. She is the editor of two critically acclaimed anthologies, *Bad Girls: 26 Writers Misbehave* and *Dirty Words: A Literary Encyclopedia of Sex*. Her website is EllenSussman.com.

When I was around forty, I wrote a novel about a happily married woman who tumbles into an affair of passion. I thought it was good, really good. So I was delighted when my agent sold it in Germany, for lots of money. But not in any other country, for some reason. For many years I thought that the Germans were just more sophisticated than everyone else.

This scene depicts the heroine doing some last-minute grocery shopping when she encounters a strangely seductive man who can't stop looking at her avocados. What could be sexier?

Looking back, I wonder if I created a new genre: vegetable erotica. *The Affair* was my first published novel. I thought I had written a great novel, not a supermarket harlequin romance. It's only now, years later, reading this with fresh eyes, that I think: Cover up those strawberries! Don't undress that cellophane! You won't find a beating heart there or anywhere else, that's for sure.

—E.S.

Jessa passed the carts at the front door, passed the hand-baskets even—she only needed strawberries. There were very few people in the supermarket—it was too late for the moms and too early for the late-night stragglers.

A man was choosing avocados. Jessa stopped when she saw his hands, watched his hands turn over an avocado, reject it, choose another. His hands held the avocado for a moment and then he brought it to his nose. She looked up.

He was watching her.

"Am I in your way?" he asked.

She was surprised to be caught. She had felt invisible. "No. I'm sorry." She was about to move on and then she said, "Do they smell?"

"Here," he said, stepping toward her, holding it under her nose. She took a breath and smelled his hands.

"This one's ripe," he said, smiling. "You can have it."

She shook her head and he took his hand, the avocado, his smell away.

"I need strawberries," she said.

He was not tall, but his face was arresting; she liked his beard, his strong nose, his deep-set eyes. She liked his hands, remarkable hands.

"Do you play piano?" she asked, looking at his hands.

"No," he said, still smiling. "Only avocados."

"I need strawberries," she said again and finally she turned away.

She found them, rows of little crates, bundles of huge, bulbous strawberries pushing their way out of their cellophane covers. She stared at them stupidly and knew that the man was at her side now, was watching her choose.

"I know," she said. "I should smell them." She didn't look up but felt his arm against hers.

"No," he said and his voice was deep but very sweet. "You have to look at them. Closely."

He lifted the cellophane cover of one of the baskets, undressing it. He picked up the basket and brought it close to Jessa's face. She closed her eyes for a moment and then opened them and saw strawberries.

She looked at him.

"I like your blouse," he said.

"You mean my breasts," she said.

"Those too," he told her.

"I don't usually dress like this for the market."

"I'm glad you did."

"I'm at a party. A dinner party."

"Are you having fun?"

"Not very much."

He put the strawberries into her hands. She felt his fingers touch the edges of her palms.

"And you?" she asked.

"I'm having a great deal of fun," he said.

"Not now," she said. "Before. Before you came here."

"Before I came here I put my wife to bed early because she's got the flu and I decided I wanted an avocado."

"That's all. Just an avocado?"

"I want more than that now," he said.

"Would you like strawberries?" she asked.

"I would love strawberries," he said.

"Here. Take these," she offered, handing him the crate. But his hands were still there, next to hers, and it was as if she was putting her hands in his.

"We can share them," he suggested.

"I'm married," she said.

"I know," he told her.

"Our best friends are over for dinner and I just ran out for strawberries."

"Come with me for a walk."

"No," she said.

She looked at his eyes—were they gray or green?—and she turned away, toward the rows of strawberries, of tangerines, of lemons. Every color looked too red, too orange, too yellow in the sharp fluorescent glare. When she looked back at him he was smiling.

"You'll come with me," he said.

"Do I look like a woman who would do what you tell me to do?"

"No," he said and his fingers touched her wrist. "I like that too."

*

After cereal and toast and conversation about homework, a dinner meeting, Rosie's lost sneaker; after the girls left for school and Roger left for work, Jessa walked into her bedroom to shower and dress. But she found her blouse on the floor, her transparent blouse from the night before, and when she picked it up and held it to her face, she smelled the stranger.

She took off her nightshirt and held the blouse in front of her. She looked in the mirror. Now she could see her breasts, the curve of them, the soft slope of them, the nipples darker, harder, more insistent. She could see everything through the thin material of the shirt—she could see the man's hand choosing her breast the way he chose an avocado, taking her nipple to his mouth the way he tasted a strawberry. And through the sheer fabric, she could see the beating of her heart.

COPING

HEATHER DONAHUE

HEATHER DONAHUE starred in the film *The Blair Witch Project*, and has appeared in many films and television shows since, including a guest role on the sitcom *It's Always Sunny in Philadelphia*. She is author of the memoir *Growgirl: The Blossoming of an Unlikely Outlaw*, about her time as a medical marijuana grower.

//

I wrote "Coping" when I was eleven, and in sixth grade. In the interest of the TMI version of twenty-first-century honesty, I did later go to therapy in California for a total of four weeks with an incredibly hot therapist. I finally ended the therapy by saying, "You know, I kind of feel like you're my ear hooker and I want to have more respect for your profession." He looked a lot like Jordan in the story you're about to read.

This was written for a class assignment, circa 1985. It was carefully bound and preserved by my parents.

—H.D.

"Kim, slow down, you are going too fast,"
shrieked Kara as she saw the speedometer accelerating
50, 60, then 70 miles per hour. "Please slow down,"
came desperate cries from Kara. "Shut up and enjoy the
ride," said Kim. Her breath was a very putrid com-
bination of beer, whiskey and vodka, "Let me out,"
cried Kara.

But then it was too late. Kims 83' chevy was
totaled. It ran into a street lamp. There lay Kara
in the middle of the wreck, blood oozing from her
head and lip. "No, Kara I'm so sorry please talk to
me, please don't die you're all I've got, I need
you," lamented Kim. Kim just sat there, her head on
Kara's blood soaked chest. "No! No! No!" exclaimed
Kim almost commanding Kara not to die and leave her
all alone. "Goodbye Kara," whispered Kim, hardly
able to speak, as she walked away. There were sirens
in the distance, as much as she didn't want to leave
Kara she also didn't want to get caught on charges
of underage drinking and drunk driving. She had
felt so vulnerable at that moment, all she could do
was drop down and cry out of helplessness.

Kim never told anyone about this so they all
figured that Kara was borrowing Kim's car and just
went out of control. Kim did not say this was a lie,
yet she didn't say it was true either. The effect of
keeping this all to herself increased the drug problem she already had. Her mother realized that she
was acting rather strangely but thought it was just
from the shock of Kara's death.

Kim spent a few days in solitude until her
mother told her that it was time to go back to
school. Kim tried this for one day but couldn't
do it. So she just walked the streets for seven
hours.

Three days later was Kara's funeral. When Kim saw Kara's parents she felt anguished and ashamed because Kara's family thought Kara died of her own driving accident.

Later, about a day Kim collapsed in the bathroom after a suicide attempt.

"Idon't deserve to live,"called Kim.

"Yes you do," cried a voice from the base of the stairs; her mother was home on lunch and came in just enough time to hear Kim's cries for help. Her mother immediately got on the phone with the local drug rehabilitation center. They said to bring her down right away.

"I'm Not going anywhere."

"Yes you are."

"Please don't make me go."

"Don't you want help?"

"No, well yes but I don't deserve it, I don't want to be better when I know Kara won't."

"I understand how you feel but"

"No you don't, no one does. Did you ever kill your best friend?"

"You killed her?"

"Yes, I killed her what more do you want from me?"

"I want you to go to the center."

"I can't I really wish I could but do you realize the guilt I'd feel."

"No, but there are people at the center that do and you know that Kara would want you to get help."

"Okay I'll try it but I can't promise that I'll stay."

"Fair enough."

"Hi Kim, I'm Jordan and I'll be your social worker and hopefully your friend here at the center."
"Hi," replied Kim almost speechless by Jordan and his kindness, warmth, exquisite blue eyes, radiant smile, golden blond hair and a captivating, creamy clear complexion.
"Well Kim why don't we have our first session today?"
"Okay."
"How old are you Jordan?"
"I'm twenty."
"Really? I'm seventeen," said Kim, wondering if the enchantment was mutual. "Well Jordan I was wondering well if you were going out with anybody like, serious and all."
"Well actually just broke up why?"
"Well if you think it would be okay could we have our first session tonight like over dinner or something."
"I think thats a fine idea what time should I pick you up?"
"How about seven-thirty?"
"Sure, see ya then, okay." Kim was squealing with delight for the first time in months. It made her disheartened in a way though, that Kara wouldn't be there to share the experience with her. But she decided on doing the next best thing, go to the cemetary after all if it wasn't for Kara she wouldn't have met Jordan.

"Hi Kara," she said to the headstone as tears began to drip down her face. "Great news, I met this social worker at the drug rehabilitation center his name is Jordan and he's only twenty and guess what? I asked him if we could have our first session over dinner tonight and he said yes; He's picking me up at seven-thirty, I'll come tommorrow and tell you all the details." "See ya tommorrow,"she said, with a smile.

&stream

That night Jordan came right at seven-thirty.
He looked really great. He was wearing a tweed suit
with his hair combed to the side. Of course Kim
looked quite special herself considering she was
going out with Jordan.
"Where are we going," said Kim.
"How about the Country Inn?"
"Sure"
"Bye Mom"
"Bye Kim have a nice time."
"I will."
As they walked to the car Jordan asked,"How's it
going?"
"Not to well."
"Why?"
"Well so far this month I killed my best friend not
to mention only friend; I tried two suicidal attempts
yet the worst part was I had to keep it all to my-
self." Kim whispered this as tears streamed down
her face. Part of her didn't want Jordan to see
her like this but the other half didn'treally care.
"Why did you have to keep it to yourself?"
"Because if anybody knew I'd be in big trouble."
"You'd still have to go to Juvenile Court but it
wouldn't be that bad, the worst is over."
"But if Kara's parents knew."
"We'll deal with that later."
"Thanks Jordan, you will never know how glad I am
to have you here helping me survive this mess I
call my life."
"Gee thanks thats quite a compliment."replied Jordan,
jokingly. Now Kim was laughing too. It felt so good
since she hadn't laughed in such a long time. It
felt so good like she'd done something that she
never thought she'd do again, like someone thats
terrified of heights going skydiving. Being with
Jordan was an odd feeling for Kim but not odd in
a bad way, odd in a sensational way. By the end of
dinner Kim could tell that the attraction was mutual
and she thought how great it was that her suicide
attempts didn't work.

As time went on Kim and Jordans relationship grew and Kim continued to make frequent trips to the cemetary to visit Kara to tell her of the latest news. As for juvenile court the Judge decided that Kim had suffered enough emotionally but still sentenced her to three weeks in a juvenile detention center and a severe warning that if she was ever caught intoxicated her sentence would be much worse.

Four years later Kim and Jordan were marriied and now own and run a teen psychology center. They also have one child, Kara, so the first Kara will never be forgotten.

NOUS

GLEN DAVID GOLD is the author of two novels, *Carter Beats the Devil* and *Sunnyside*. His essays, memoirs, and short fiction have appeared in *McSweeney's*, the *New York Times Magazine*, and the *Independent UK*. He lives in the San Francisco Bay Area.

I lay the blame for "Nous" at the feet of Philip Glass. In the summer of 1979, I was living in a New York apartment. I was sixteen. My radio got only one station after midnight, from some university (NYU? Columbia?). One night, I thought the radio had gotten stuck somehow on the same couple of measures. But then, no, the driving piano and synthesizer and sax and whatever else was trapped in there had changed. Then it changed again.

Half-awake, I couldn't tell how long had passed. It was a nightmare. I hated this music. But then I needed to know what it was. Ten minutes later, it was still going and like a lot of high school hates, I realized I loved it. And out came the pen, unfortunately. I remembered a class about the three parts of Platonic love—and so I wrote "Eros" and "Thumos," salutes to passion and the desire for the intangible. Neither one of which is nearly as terrible as the third poem, "Nous," which describes "mental desire." The poems were published in *Symposium*, the literary journal of the Thacher School.

When the music ended, I learned I'd been listening to "Dances No. 1 and 3" off of an as-yet-unreleased tape by Philip Glass, and I had a poem in front of me that I just knew was my ticket to being a part of the creative avant-garde.

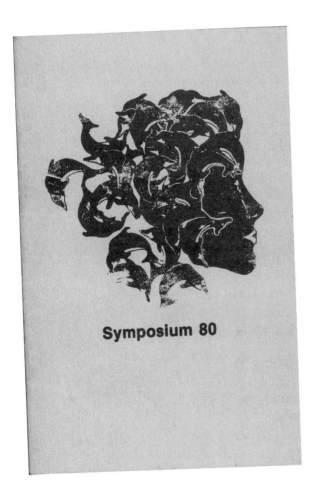

Symposium 80

I cringe particularly at the "pons more alluring than mons" line, because I thought that marked me as above all the lust stuff. Once I finally got acquainted with one of those mons things, all that high moral crap flew out the window. I don't even know what a "hazelrod harlequin" is, but it sounds like a piece of melty candy and I wouldn't let it anywhere near a mons.

—G.D.G.

NOUS

The Bright pink sweetmeat in the melancholy grey voice, She is.

        Ringed with   Rhinestones

        Rare as Radium

        Is the elegant beauty

Lover . . . love her apple of your sweet eyeteeth

Aorta becoming more than areola

Pons more alluring than mons

Her harmonious contour attracts only after she as.

Hair of liquid gold, a sun's brightest day, the majesty of

          Lion's price—

Skin of polished cedar, yet soft as sea foam—

Iris of breakfast sky, pool velvet and doe's tail—

A Hazelrod Harlequin.

Oh, god-goddess—it hurts.

            So beautiful—so dangerous.

            Gelt upon Love upon Pain upon Pain
            upon Pain

            The masque on Beauty of Beauty
            Underneath—

            A painful, festering wound

            Wrinkled and Pink

            To heal, you require cure—

            Her, to fill the fleshy caverns of the
            heart and minds.

SUSAN STRAIGHT

HIGH SCHOOL BOYS

Straight and her future husband.

SUSAN STRAIGHT has published eight novels, including the Rio Seco trilogy: *Between Heaven and Here*, *Take One Candle Light a Room*, and *A Million Nightingales*. *Highwire Moon* was a finalist for the National Book Award in 2001. In April 2014, Straight received the Robert Kirsch Award for Lifetime Achievement from the *Los Angeles Times*. Her short stories have appeared in *Zoetrope*, the *Ontario Review*, the *Oxford American*, the *Sun*, *Black Clock*, and elsewhere. Her essays have appeared in the *New York Times*, *Reader's Digest*, *Family Circle*, *Salon*, the *Los Angeles Times*, *Harper's*, the *Nation*, and other magazines.

///

I was almost fourteen, one day older than my best friend, Tami, and we'd met some guys who were high school seniors. Nobody broke my heart, but someone broke hers, and then I decided to be heartbroken too. So I wrote this poem for us, on the rebound.

I wrote twelve poems, some worse than others. This one might be the worst. I thought everything had to rhyme, clearly, and it made Tami feel better. A few weeks later, I met my future husband on a school bus trip to the Los Angeles Zoo, where my classmates were so obnoxious to the primates that our freshman class was kicked out of the zoo. Seriously.

On the bus ride home, he and I started talking. The photo was taken when we were eighteen, and I was a freshman again—at USC this time.

—S.S.

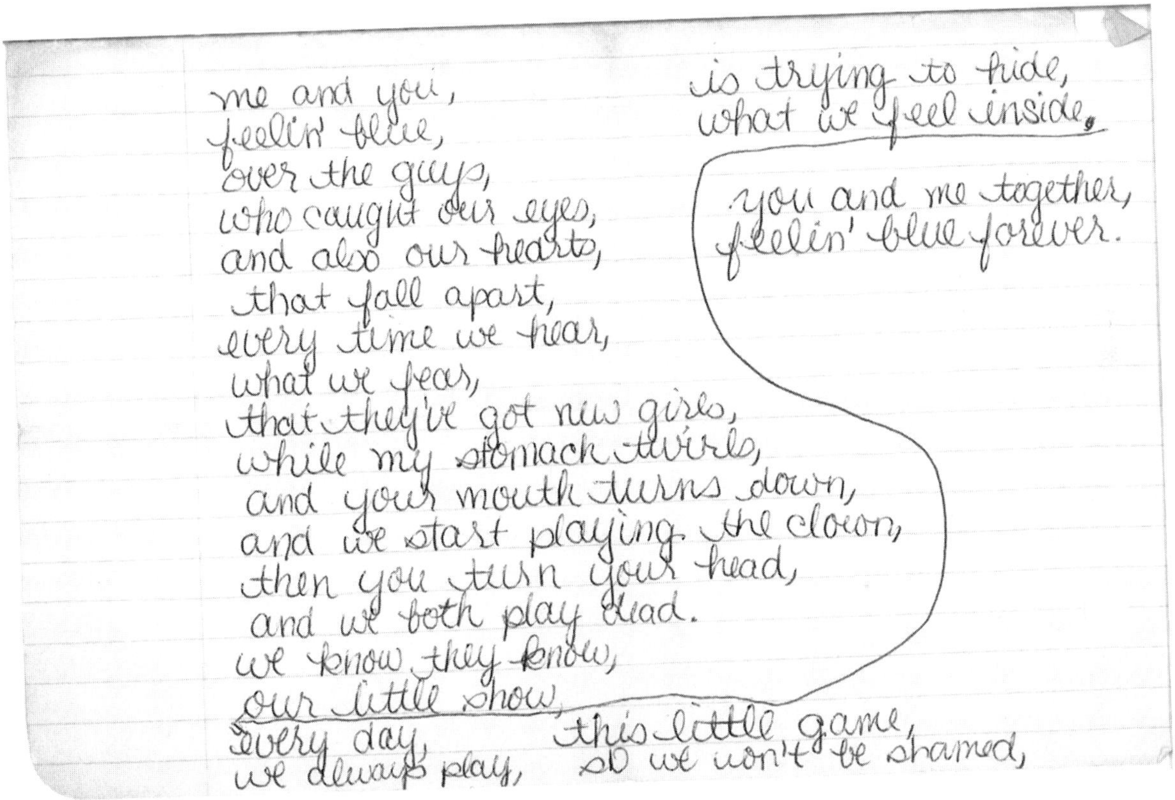

me and you,
feelin' blue,
over the guys,
who caught our eyes,
and also our hearts,
that fall apart,
every time we hear,
what we fear,
that they've got new girls,
while my stomach twirls,
and your mouth turns down,
and we start playing the clown,
then you turn your head,
and we both play dead.
we know, they know,
our little show,
every day,   this little game,
we always play,   so we won't be shamed,
is trying to hide,
what we feel inside,
you and me together,
feelin' blue forever.

RASPY ROMANCE

LAURA FRASER is the author of the memoirs *An Italian Affair* and *All Over the Map*, as well as a long-time journalist and the recent cofounder and editorial director of Shebooks, which publishes short ebooks by women.

When I was sixteen, my friend Sallie was addicted to bodice-ripping romances. I teased her about it—especially since I had to write her *Great Gatsby* paper because she'd been too busy reading *Love's Tender Fury*. I told her romance novels were so trashy even I could write one. So, for her seventeenth birthday, I did.

Raspy Romance, from a literary point of view, has a few problems. For one thing, there is no beach near Denver, where the hero, Brent Donovan, takes the raven-haired Mollie to proclaim the ardor of his affections while pressing his manhood against her. For another, it's not quite clear what exactly happens on that beach when slowly, tenderly, they enact the promise of true love. At sixteen, the whole notion of sex—and "manhood" in particular—was vague, to say the least, and my imagination lurked in the great, confusing void between romantic comedies and my mother's copy of *Everything You Always Wanted to Know About Sex But Were Afraid to Ask.*

Some excerpts follow.

—L.F.

ONE DAY as Mollie finished a song at the tavern, she tripped as she went down the two rickety stairs to the stage. Her foot was caught between two slats. No one in the smoke-filled room paid attention to her cries. The clattering of beer mugs and shouts of the poker game were too loud to distinguish her voice from the squeals of drunken hussies.

Frustrated and in pain, Mollie's foot throbbed as it was stuck between the boards. Then she felt relief when two strong arms gently pried the boards apart. Then he picked her up, carried her to the lobby, and set her on the couch, and propped her foot up on his lap. Mollie smiled gratefully into his deep blue eyes.

She was awed by his appearance, more distinguished, yet rugged and handsome than any man she had ever seen, even in England. He was tall and broad, though slim. The fine linen of his loose, embroidered shirt could scarcely hide the rippling muscles of his arms. His rich brown hair was feathered back to expose a tanned face with a determined and prominent jaw.

"You've got to be careful, miss," he said tenderly as he looked at her ankle with concern. He laughed softly. "You'll be fine, though. It doesn't seem like even a sore ankle could slow you down," he said, noticing how her compact little body squirmed on the sofa.

Mollie smiled at him. She chatted easily with him; his warm humor made him enjoyable to talk to.

"My name is Brent," he said. "Brent Donovan. I'm from Denver, out here on business. Now do you think, if I helped you, you might be able to make it to dinner with me?"

[. . .]

Brent and Mollie walked slowly along the beach talking. They came upon a secluded spot, surrounded by trees. They sat down on a large rock, facing the moon over the ocean.

In the moonlight, Mollie appeared more enchanting than ever. Her face was silhouetted against the rock, surrounded by the darkness of her loose hair. Her eyes reflected Brent as he looked at her; his face was open and sincere. To Mollie, his was a face of unprecedented charm.

Brent's large, hard body kept her warm, his sinewy muscles enveloping her and he placed his sturdy hands upon her waist. As he looked into her eyes, he leaned towards her, kissing her gently. She could scarcely feel the difference between the kiss and the wind brushing her lips. He kissed her again, and lingered. The moments passed, binding their love irrevocably.

He gathered Mollie in his arms, carefully laying her down on the soft, fine sand. His blue eyes were soft, in contrast to the hardness of his face. When he removed his shirt, Mollie caressed the smoothness of his chest and the broad expanse of his shoulders. He kissed her more passionately as the ruffled skirt and peasant blouse slipped off her body, leaving her in her sheer lace shift.

Softly he kissed her breasts, and softly his hand explored her warm, enraptured body. Trembling to his touch, she kissed him with fervor and felt his body responding. Then, naturally and tenderly, but with the ardency of desire, their bodies met. It was the celebration of true love.

THE END

(unless you prefer to use your imagination)

LETTER TO MUSTACHE
(AFTER MICHAEL ONDAATJE)

MELANIE GIDEON

MELANIE GIDEON is the author of the memoir *The Slippery Year: A Meditation on Happily Ever After*, an NPR and San Francisco Chronicle Best Book of 2009. Her novel *Wife 22* has been translated into thirty languages and is currently in development with Working Title Films.

W hen I was in my twenties, I was in a relationship with a man I'll call Mustache. We'd been dating a long time and our relationship was on its last legs but neither one of us could summon up the courage to end it. It was one of those addictive, obsessive sort of loves. Lots of drama. Jealous rages. Everything life and death all the time.

So, while this drama was going on I had just discovered Michael Ondaatje's novel *In the Skin of a Lion*. I carried the book around with me like a talisman. The novel was full of gravitas and, to me, unbelievably sexy and erotic. Short, lyrical sentences, fragmentary, almost like a poem. It was haunting. And I was not the only one who felt that way.

Anne Enright wrote in the *Guardian*: "There are certain books that should be taken away from young writers; that should be prised out of their clutching fingers and locked away until they are all grown up and ready to read them without being smitten. At the very least, they should have 'Don't try this on your own typewriter' printed in bold across the front. *In the Skin of a Lion* is full of things that Michael Ondaatje can do, but that you probably can't do, or can't do yet. It is a highly contagious book."

Contagious, yes. I ignored Ms. Enright's advice; I did indeed try this on my own typewriter. So, circa 1986, Michael Ondaatje *In the Skin of a Lion*–inspired, I give to you—a love letter to Mustache.

—M.G.

On the road. By a river. Running through mazes of green. You are in front of me. I lose you.

Night. Foggy. On the road. By the water. It is warm. Muggy. Hard to see. Climb over hills. Through jungles. Into darkened shacks. Through windows. Searching for you.

Finally come to the ocean. Sound of water over stone.
It is getting light.

And then I know. You are out there on the rocks.

Huge boulders with sea gushing into crevice. Searching, searching for some sign. Some difference among the boulders. Something that will tell me you are there.

I see silver bullets in the sand.

And there you are. On a rock. A ledge. On your back.

Shot through the head.

Naked. The whiteness of your body a perverse contrast to the steady brown of the stone.

You are dying. And I have never loved you more.

I reach out to you. Touch your face. Whisper your name. You open your eyes. Say my name. Smile. Your eyes are the color of bottle green glass washed up by the tide.

I am aware of the strength of my feelings. Seeing you vulnerable on the rock. Unprotected from cold. Wind. Water. The feeling is so intense I see it as a color. Gold. Deep, swirling gold. Flows from the hand down through the fingertips to where I touch your face.

And although I know there are other bodies out there on the rocks besides yours, I don't move. Don't want to move. Don't care about them.

Just want to be near. And touch you in your weakness. And be the name you call when you open your eyes and feel the cold slab of stone underneath your back.

And remember where you are.

LOVE POEM FOR A TRUE HIPPIE

JANE GANAHL has been a journalist, author, teacher, editor, and arts producer in San Francisco for thirty years. She is the cofounder and codirector of Litquake, the West Coast's largest independent literary festival. She is also the author of the memoir *Naked on the Page: The Misadventures of My Unmarried Midlife*, and editor of the anthology *Single Woman of a Certain Age*. She has contributed essays to five anthologies and has written for *Salon*, *Vanity Fair*, *Rolling Stone*, *Ladies' Home Journal*, *Huffington Post*, *Harper's Bazaar*, and many more. She is unfortunate in that much of her early newspaper work is archived.

The first and only writing group I ever belonged to was a loose one created in 1967 with friends in high school for the purposes of sharing our embryonic attempts at the written word. I was fifteen. One friend specialized in short love stories featuring Neil Young as her paramour. My specialty was poetry. I started with hippie-eco-warrior tomes—my favorite poem blasted the county for paving a freeway through the bucolic hills I lived in—and moved on from there to poems about my crushes.

I went looking for my folder of teen poems recently and was pleasantly surprised that, while gushy and shallow as teenage girls are, they have a nice dramatic tension to them, and a definite Honors English vocabulary. This one was written for a guy named Bill Spangler, who reminded me of Peter Tork of the Monkees and was in all the school plays. He was, with long hair and tattered jeans, a True Hippie—compared to this aspiring one—and I would swoon when he walked by and deigned to smile. The hot album of the year was Jefferson Airplane's *Surrealistic Pillow*, which provided the soundtrack to both that tumultuous political time and to my love life, or what passed for it. The *Pillow* song "How Do You Feel" spoke to the writer's anguish at being tongue-tied when encountering a crush: "Oh, how my heart beats, I don't even think I can talk . . ." Exactly.

—J.G.

```
on that too-rare
occasion
when he bends down
to give me
a smile,
my poor, starving mind
reels
and the rest of the world
slips into
oblivion.
upon glimpsing that
beautiful
hairy head
bobbing through the crowd
my mental strings
tintinambulate
to the melody of
"How do you feel", and
i fall into
the gutter.
i'm sorry.
i'm not ignoring you.
He is the
only one
i can see.
```

3

ILL-ADVISED CONFESSIONS

The man of my dreams, that restless feminist whom I could love without boundaries: where is he?

—Julia Scheeres

LETTER TO THE DRAFT BOARD

TODD OPPENHEIMER

TODD OPPENHEIMER works as a journalist at the Writers' Grotto, a San Francisco collective for freelance writers, filmmakers, and others devoted to the narrative arts. Oppenheimer has written for a variety of newspapers and magazines such as the *New Yorker*, the *Atlantic*, *Newsweek*, the *Washington Post*, and the *New York Times*. He has received multiple national awards for his writing, including a first prize from Investigative Reporters and Editors (IRE), and a National Magazine Award for public interest reporting for "The Computer Delusion," a 1997 cover story Oppenheimer wrote for the *Atlantic*. He is the author of *The Flickering Mind: Saving Education from the False Promise of Technology*, which was a finalist for IRE's investigative book award.

//

In the fall of 1971, when I was nineteen and in my first year of college, living in a high-rise dorm at UC Berkeley, I got a notice that I was up for being drafted into the Vietnam War. This meant that I, an innocent preppie, might have to join hordes of America's teenagers in an adventure that, let's just say, I was not exactly cut out for. This, I could not tolerate. So I sought the only escape that seemed feasible: I filed for deferment as a conscientious objector to the war.

I also got a lawyer—a bright young man whose father was our family rabbi. My next task was to write a brilliant essay. I had to prove that I had a long-standing religious belief system, or some equivalent set of deeply held moral values, which rendered me incapable of engaging in war—of any kind.

No problem. That winter, I sent the draft board fifteen neatly typed pages, which went into my feelings—in full. In the interests of space, I will restrict myself to a few excerpts, as follows.

The nature of my anti-war beliefs is based on a deep respect for the magic in humanity that has been brought out by my main interest in life. This interest of mine is the Theatre. I spent this past summer in the American Conservatory Theater's Training Program, right here in San Francisco. It is from the personal interactions that I watched and went through at ACT that my beliefs about human beings were strengthened and clarified.

After an actor has explored the internal processes of characters he has represented, he is soon rather taken with the magic and wonder of the human spirit that is literally impossible to kill with any sort of indifference. This demand that acting requires of you has led to me to discover, enjoy and respect that part of human beings that is much too beautiful to kill with such warlike indifference.

Since I attended ACT, I have come to value, above all, the richness of human emotion. An actor, at an early stage in his training, is often told to observe people. For a while, I had to consciously remember to do this. But for about a month now, I have found it an automatic part of me.

I feel that my experience with the intensely alert

and dedicated artists at ACT has been a religious
training; a training that has gelled my religious
convictions. These religious beliefs have given me a
love and concern for the magical part of human beings
that acting explores. And if one loves that in humans,
then how can one kill a man with whom he's never even
shared knowledge of each other's souls? For surely if
you are going to kill a man you ought to have had time
to explore that man's internal life, therefore having
at least developed a fairly justified hate and then
still have a very good reason to say in essence, that
you are more deserving of a place on earth than he is.

People are far too worthy of personal and spiritual
exploration to go through a war destroying those whose
spirits have so much to offer. I do not believe you
can even lightly judge a man, much less kill him, if
you never even took the time to know him and find out
his personal values. War is a judgment—war is not
self-defense.

. . .

To me, this seemed argument-proof. When I showed this essay to my lawyer, he paused, nodded sagely, and said, "Who knows? It might work. It's different."

A few months later, I got a letter from the draft board, with a card inside that was marked 4F—a medical deferment. I immediately drove to my lawyer's office to give him the news. We both whooped it up. And then, just as I was leaving, I asked him what chance he thought I'd really have had with my conscientious objector application. Without a moment's thought he put his right hand out and gestured, thumb down. "Whoa," I said. "Why?!" He looked at me for a minute, and then he said, "Because, at this point in the war, the draft board is sick of educated Jewish kids who can afford a lawyer."

—T.O.

EAT WHAT YOU KILL

PO BRONSON has authored seven bestselling works of nonfiction and fiction. He has won nine national awards, including the PEN USA Award for Literary Journalism and the American Association for the Advancement of Science Award for Outstanding Journalism. He is a founder of the San Francisco Writers' Grotto.

I wish I could use the first-pancake excuse, but I can't. For this wasn't my first attempt at a novel. That first one, written longhand into spiral journals on a West 87th Street couch, was at least in the genre of domestic realism. A love story set in the Manhattan art world, my tale was unreadable but it was not unmentionable. At parties, I could describe the book in ways that made it sound vaguely compelling.

Nor was I naive about that first one: 125 pages into typing it up on an old typewriter, I came to a cold stop. I stretched a rubber band around the belly of the manuscript and buried the thing deep in a drawer. It was time to go get a job, a real job. I told myself I'd come back to it in a few months, which became a few years. I don't regret that one; I'm actually proud of the fact I was wise enough to cache it like a time capsule and disentangle myself from its faux ambitions.

But this one, my second one, has me grasping for excuses. Rereading its overstuffed sentences, I wonder if it had something to do with the Macintosh.

Remember when the Mac arrived, and you could not only edit sentences ad infinitum, but you could lend prose some persuasion through the careful choice of typeface? You could give your sentences that Garamondian flavor. Hushed sincerity could be imparted with the angled strokes of italic! Poor wordsmithing could be covered up by making it look intentional with a little Old Antiqua here and there. Those were the days . . .

My sentences, though. Each a contraption. Only the sort of thing that could be constructed with the benefit of the word processor. It was as if I were being paid extra for every adverb, and double bonus for every run-on.

Here's just the opening line:

Leaves parachuting from delicate limbs breathing and stretching and swaying in autumn rhythms, dancing as they fall this fall in tune to winds and the gentle breezes from the top of the mountain.

The whole 230-page novel is like that. I was working on Wall Street at the time, in bond sales. This novel was the Opposite World I escaped to every night. By day, I barked numbers into squawk boxes. At night, I penned lyrics of prose. By day, I was on the forty-second floor of a downtown glass tower, surrounded by electronic screens on all sides. By night, I vanished into the setting of my novel: the forest.

Oh, and all my characters were animals. Here's the list of characters, from the frontispiece:

List of Characters

Darmot, a marmot, the defendant

Weasel, the prosecutor

Raven, a vulture, the judge

Nyrpatta, Darmot's younger brother

Tumratha, Darmot's wife

Wolverine

Pika, a small rabbit

Capira, a lynx and Nyrpatta's friend

Otta, a river otter

Goby, a pocket gopher

Tharnyx, a falcon

Capira's father

The jury

Yes, it was a legal thriller, a courtroom drama. It was Scott Turow à la *Watership Down*. It was *Animal Farm*, but rather than on a farm—the Rockies!

The conceit was that a marmot had behaved not very marmotly. Marmots are basically big squirrels who whistle. Marmots are not predators. Sure, they'll steal a bird egg. But they're cuddly nut hunters. Not beasts. No tooth and claw.

This particularly intelligent marmot had murdered in revenge, intentionally, using poison and trickery. He had upset the Natural Order of Things. So he was being brought to justice. That was the grandiose theme of my grandiose novel: Was it wrong for an herbivore to go all savage now and then?

A friend at the investment bank asked to read it. A few weeks later, I asked him if he'd started it. "Oh yes," he said. "It's the best book about Wall Street I've ever read."

Now, the most embarrassing part: I didn't just write one draft. I put the book through three separate drafts over the next eighteen months. Every time, I had the chance to back away; instead I doubled down on my investment. In fact, that year of rewriting is the stick by which I measure wasted time. When I duck into a pizza place, hoping for a quick slice, and after handing over my money I learn it's going to take ten minutes to bake it—I cast back to my second novel. When I think about that girlfriend I should have broken up with, I indelibly call to mind my second novel. When I think about flying home for Christmas, only to do nothing but watch TV and eat—I ponder the even greater waste that was my second novel.

I used the manuscript to get admitted to the creative writing program at San Francisco State. I thought at State I would hone the novel to the point of publishing glory. But the first day of school, I had a meeting with the program director. He read aloud to me from the first page of my manuscript:

> Slipping under fallen branches, some broken arm of a friendly spruce, soaring over sorrel and laurel, like a fish I once saw in the water, jumping over every several steps above the breast of the water, flying for a second like a great kingfisher pelican, swimming the next like a steelhead salmon.

"You know what you need to do with this novel? I recommend you put it in a drawer for a year or two. Come back to it then, if you feel like it."

—P.B.

I DREAM OF WARM PLACES

PETER ORNER is the author of two novels, *Love and Shame and Love* and *The Second Coming of Mavala Shikongo*, and two story collections, *Last Car Over the Sagamore Bridge* and *Esther Stories*. Orner's stories and essays have appeared in the *Atlantic*, the *New York Times*, the *San Francisco Chronicle*, the *Paris Review*, *Granta*, *McSweeney's*, the *Believer*, the *Southern Review*, and elsewhere. His work has been anthologized in *The Best American Short Stories* and *The Best American Nonrequired Reading* and twice won a Pushcart Prize. He is also the editor of two nonfiction books, *Underground America* and *Hope Deferred: Narratives of Zimbabwean Lives*. Orner is a professor of creative writing at San Francisco State University.

//

Not only don't I really recognize the person who wrote the stuff that follows, but I'm not sure I ever knew this guy at all, which sounds weird because it's me, my handwriting, my little narrow-ruled notebook from the early 1990s—and yet as I read it, this notebook I'd been hauling around with me for years, and not to get all heavy here, but I felt the weight of the years in my own goofy-ass prose. We die not one death but hundreds. Who is this poor idiot sitting at the McDonald's eating a McLean Deluxe and spouting off nonsense?

Why anybody else would want to read this, God knows. For a few sporadic months back in 1992, I kept a journal. It was the only time in my life I ever did.

I got bored of my own dopey thoughts and gave it up soon after. What I've wanted, what I've always wanted, is to inhabit the thoughts of other people, which is why I take a little bit of solace in that, as interested as I am below in myself, I also spend time watching and thinking about the meter maid and the bearded man. Kill me if I ever write a memoir.

I was waiting tables in Cambridge, Massachusetts. The restaurant was in a mall out in East Cambridge and, if I remember, was called Rayz Riverside Café, a crappy place with a lot of neon and sad razzle-dazzle, kind of like a slightly more upscale TGI Friday's. Eventually, I got fired, and I remember stomping off into the snow with an apron full of cash and credit card receipts. I considered it my unemployment compensation. But at the time I wrote this stuff I was still working there and on a break and apparently slipped out to McDonald's for lunch, which strikes me as odd since I worked in a restaurant.

—P.O.

Oct 13, 1992:

In a McDonald's with fifteen minutes to tell my hopes and dreams and fears. I suddenly feel very weighted down by this McLean Deluxe. A bearded man who looks like a little a white Fredrick Douglass just struggled up to me and asks me I had a smoke. No smokes, I said. The manager is trying to toss him out right now. At least the guy knows what he wants, a cigarette. That's what he craves. At the moment I am not nearly as focused. I crave money. I crave adventure. I crave respect. Power and finally when it all comes down to it love. A parking enforcement officer just sat down in the next booth. She must be a regular because she keeps greeting everybody by name. I have never seen anything like this, people being so friendly to a meter maid. They must not own cars. Anyway. I find it difficult to write about myself directly. And who can write about love without it sounding like a cliché. But I find it difficult to imagine that anything could be better than decent, honest, actual love. Honesty I guess that's something I crave also. So when I do discover this love I seem to crave, I will for once become honest to her and myself. In the meantime I will continue to search for something to cling to in my life. The parking officer is back. She is talking on her walkie talkie and blowing into her hands to keep warm. I fear death but I guess this is natural. But I also fear becoming ordinary, perhaps even more than I fear death, I fear averageness, I fear not making a mark, fear dying without accomplishment. But who is the judge? The bearded man just called the manager "a fucking yuppie with your fucking tie!" The manager just jumped on the bearded man's foot. These two could go at it for hours. It's a standoff. The bearded man isn't budging. The manager is standing with his hands on his hips. Here come the cops. They're going to take him to the Pine Street Inn. He's walking with a limp now. He says he was hit by a car. The bearded man leaves. I stay. The manager is satisfied. The parking lady begins to nod off. Chilled by the opening of the door, I dream of warm places.

ELIZABETH BERNSTEIN

BIRTH OF A FLOWER

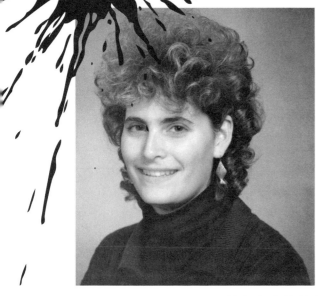

ELIZABETH BERNSTEIN lives in the San Francisco Bay Area. She founded and edited the *Big Ugly Review*, an online literary magazine, and her short stories have been published in the *Los Angeles Times Magazine*, the *San Francisco Bay Guardian* (fiction contest winner), *Tin House*, the *North American Review*, and other U.S. and international literary journals. She's a freelance book editor at EBC-Books.com.

It was 1986. I was nineteen years old, a sophomore in college. I rocked a Demi Moore haircut (circa *St. Elmo's Fire*)—short around the ears, frosted on top. All through that long, cold New England winter, I lay on my dorm room bed, listening to Roxy Music, Spandau Ballet, and the Fixx on an endless loop, waiting for spring to come.

And then, one day, it did. The ice melted; the grass grew; the sun came out. Everything was starting to blossom.

Even me.

I had always been a late bloomer. I entered high school at four-foot-ten, and five years later, I had grown nine inches. What was this new body? Who was this young woman? All I knew was that I was no longer a girl. Things were going to happen for me now. Big things. Woman things.

I was enthralled. I knew just what to do to commemorate this momentous occasion, this transition from girlhood to womanhood. I rose delicately from my dorm room bed, hushed Steve Winwood's "Higher Love" on the boom box, and opened up my spiral notebook.

—E.B.

Birth of a Flower

Birth of a flower
    Awakening of spring.
        Awakening of a flower

Birth of a sun.
    Melting of water
        Dripping of ice.

Thawing of green
    Freezing of blue.

Parting of clouds
    Stirring of wind.
        Blowing of air
            Cooling of skin.

Breathing of risk
    Temptation dawns.
        Eyes awaken
            Perceive the wind.

Aware of the flower.
    Feel the green
        Taste the blue.

Lick the earth
    Kiss the sun.

Birth of a flower
    Awakening of spring.
    Taste of life
        End of dream.

Thawing of winter
    Birth of a soul.

Birth of a flower
    Awakening of spring.

PAUL REISER'S GHOST:
A DREAM JOURNAL

ZAHRA NOORBAKHSH is a stand-up comedian and writer-performer of two national shows, *All Atheists Are Muslim* and *Hijab and Hammerpants*. Her performances have sold out theaters in New York, Los Angeles, and San Francisco. Noorbakhsh's writing is featured in *Love, InshAllah: The Secret Love Lives of American Muslim Women*. Noorbakhsh is one-third of the theater troupe DISoriented, a trio of Asian American performers. As a comedian, she was a finalist in the Aspen Rooftop National College Comedy Competition and has performed with international acts such as Maz Jobrani and Shazia Mirza.

///

When I was twenty-two, I took a dream analysis class at a local junior college, because I thought it would make me psychic and I wanted to be able to tell the future. Every morning in 2002, I woke up, grabbed my pen, flung open my dream journal, and chronicled my subconscious mythologies.

I took my dream analysis class very seriously.

I forgot all about these journals until I dug them up for *Drivel*. It turns out that at the dawn of the twenty-first century, I was hanging out with every celebrity in film and television in a transpersonal party called the Collective Unconscious, from 11 p.m. to 9 a.m. Pacific standard time.

Okay, so the whole point of this analysis was to look at everything as a metaphor: the celebrities, the symbols, all of the great plot twists, but I pretty much missed the point entirely. As far as my celebrity-obsessed twenty-two-year-old self was concerned, the cast of *Mad About You* was trying to send me psychic messages.

"Our psyches are linked in the collective unconscious," my teacher used to say, which, to me, meant that I had access to a massive mind-pool of primal wisdom—transcending time and space—provided I could just decode messages from Paul Reiser, Nicole Kidman, and Stockard Channing.

—Z.N.

[NOTE: I always wrote both dates—before and after falling asleep—to make sure my dream analysis teacher knew when the psychic link was open.]

```
07/27-07/28

Dream with me stalking Diane Keaton—chasing her all
around the kitchen—blood soup in the pots in the sink.
    First I've got an axe—then a huge knife, and I'm
chasing her. Sometimes, I'm Jack Nicholson. But most of
the time, I'm me.
    I'm chasing around Diane Keaton from the film "Annie
Hall"—I am Jack Nicholson from the film "The Shining."
    We're in my house, but the room seems rearranged and
my house seems backwards somehow. The location of the
kitchen, breakfast nook, family room, and my brother's
room are the same, but everything else seems eerily
different.
    My house looks like a house straight out of a
horror flick. The energy about it is thick! It's as
```

though the dead and unresolved spirits of others that I've killed are lingering about the air, angry and cheated.

There are almost shrines, sculpture-looking dead bodies of old Kings, Lords and Gods, all lining the walls, just where they meet the ceiling, seated in throned chairs, made of the same white paint and material as the walls as though they were built from the walls. They're there to really help Diane Keaton.

The spirits of these Kings, Gods and Lords are very much alive! But are trapped in these immobile, totally paralyzed bodies. Some of their eyes move as they watch me chase Diane, who is screaming and frantic, around the kitchen and to the family room.

The sink is filled with pots and pans filled with overflowing bloody water—just waterfalling (cascading) down each pot.

07/22–07/23

The dream begins at a funeral. It's Paul Reiser's funeral. I walk as though by accident into this room.

I had come from somewhere else. I open the double doors and peek my head through.

There's a priest with the white linen garb around him reading the appropriate scripture from the Bible and saying a few words about Paul.

I see it's his funeral somewhere on a board upon an easel written in thick marker. It's there and then it's gone.

It tells me that it's Paul Reiser's funeral. When I hear that it's his funeral, there are a few people that

I immediately expect to be there. Producers, writers, comedians and Helen Hunt.

I look over to my right and see her.

Then I look for his wife and his daughter and his best friend. All are together at the very bottom of this pentagon-shaped funeral parlor.

The dream cuts.

Paul Reiser and his jokes turn into this Indian guy for a second and then back again. I'm yelling at him about the comic material he's testing. None of my evaluation occurs because he's jumping around from page to page too much. I ask him to just read a paragraph but he keeps making up his own comic routine about his parents.

Then he keeps going back and forth between him and the Indian guy.

Nobody else knows that he's Paul Reiser! Everyone thinks that he's John Brown. [NOTE: *I have no idea who John Brown is.*] In the dream, I know I'm the only one who seems to know that the Ghost of Paul Reiser has reincarnated itself into the body of the man John Brown. Not even Paul Reiser knows this. I can't see the actual body of this man he's possessed because all I can see is Paul Reiser.

I wish other people knew so that they wouldn't be sad about the death of their friend.

07/16–07/17

Meg Ryan is everywhere and there's this boy who keeps talking to her on the phone. The boy is trying to get ahold of her to come on a hike with us (my hiking class.

The most interesting part about the dream I think was that, just before I woke up I from the dream, I saw a magazine with Nicole Kidman on the cover. She looks pissed. Her hair is that bright orangey red that she looks so good in. It's pulled back into a tight, really fashionable mid-way ponytail and she's making a screaming, yelling face. She's got her hands at her temples pressed firmly and frustratedly against her head.

The cover of the magazine reads: "NICOLE KIDMAN: STUFFED AWAY AND PISSED! READY TO KICK HER WAY OUT! TOM CAN'T HOLD HER BACK FOREVER! SHE'S BEEN STUFFED AWAY AND SHE IS MORE READY THAN EVER TO MAKE A COMEBACK! LOOK OUT WORLD!"

07/29–07/30

I'm in Vegas. A casino is being robbed. Andy Garcia runs out of the double doors, sees me and stops. He hands me a black leather bag and says, "Here. There's a cut. Just a gift." And then he takes off with the police chasing him down the streets that turn into Los Angeles.

Now I'm at the beach. I open his "gift." It's a bag of diamonds. Looking at them I think, "Well, they're definitely worth $100,000, but WHAT IF THEY'RE WORTH A MILLION!?"

HELLO KITTY DIARY

KATIE CROUCH is the *New York Times* bestselling author of *Girls in Trucks*, *Abroad*, and other novels. She has written for the *London Guardian*, *McSweeney's*, *Tin House*, *Slate*, *Salon*, and has a regular column on the *Rumpus* called "Missed." A MacDowell Fellow, Crouch teaches at San Francisco State University and lives in Bolinas, California.

These excerpts are taken from my Hello Kitty diary, starting when I was nine years old. At that time, I was quite convinced that I was either going to be incredibly famous or buried in clay. Either way, I felt it important to document my ninth year so that the public could study my youth.

At the time of writing this, I was living in Charleston, South Carolina. The city has grown fivefold since, but in 1981, it was a small, pretty town, where everyone knew each other and not much went unnoticed. Most of the girls at my school were blond and wore big bows in their hair. I was freckled and bookish, which is why I spent so much time pondering "popularity."

There are two people mentioned in these entries. Frances Lumpkin has grown up to be a glamorous ad woman who lives in New York. I don't know where Wood Cleveland is, but as we are now middle-aged, I figure he would welcome the belated compliment.

One name I have redacted. The reason is I once read these entries aloud while speaking at a school, and the daughter of the redacted person was, unbeknownst to me, in the audience. This was a private girls school in Charleston, and I saw the same blond girls from my youth turn and laugh at this daughter, who was the same age that I was when I wrote the entry. I saw her cheeks burn, saw the tears, and I knew so well what she was feeling I wanted to cry myself.

This was, I suppose, a brief moment of regret.

Yet, any more attention would, I knew, make things worse. So after the reading I watched her disappear down the hall, holding her face in her hands. And I concluded that regret is useless, and life is too short for useless things. She has her own redacted desires. At least I hope she does. And I am glad to still have this diary, as I now have a descendent of my own who will, someday, enjoy it.

—K.C.

November 2, 1981

My name is Katie Crouch. I'm almost 9. I have red hair. I would be a good freind (if I may say so myself). I love rock music and animals. Whoever is reading this, I hope you are a decendent or an unknown freind.

this is how I look:

my hair is red and I have freckes all over me

November 12, 1982

Cloudy

Today was okay. Dad gave me a little book to put private things in like who my boyfriend is. I have a big crush on a 13-year-old boy whose name is Michael Wise. I think he likes me, too. I hope so! Everyone else hates hime so I guess I'm in good shape.

November 28, 1983

Warm & breezy

This is a very confusing time of life for me. Whoever is reading this, I will try to sort things out for you. To begin with: boys. A couple of boys show intrest in me, but no one is fighting for me. There is this girl in my class called Frances Lumpkin, and every boy I know likes her. She's really pretty, careless + fun to be with. Her mom owns a store called the Dandylion + it's the most fashionable store in Charlestown. She has the best clothes but couldn't care less. And she has kissed a lot of boys. I've only kissed one! And he was related to me.

Second of all: growing up. You might call me "an early maturer." I'm only 10 + in 5th grade + I already need a bra badly + have lots of hair you-know-where. I know I will get my period soon, but I'm scared of getting it, I hope it doesn't ever happen!

March 16, 1984
Sunny & warm

I am so happy! I have figured out a way to be popular! The girls are liking me a lot more than they used to! This is my way:

Don't ever say something mushy.

Never say yes.

Act careless.

January 24, 1985

Dear Diary,

It has been a year since I wrote to you! In the past, I've said some pretty stupid things. Also, in the first of the diary, I was pretty problemless! But that's all part of growing up. Now, I'm 11, but I think like an 18-year-old. I'm pretty intelligent, my friends say. No one in my class hates me.

I like a boy named W♥♥d Cleveland! (sigh!)

He's in 5th grade, has brown hair and green eyes with green specks. Also, he has a toothy grin and a mole under his nose. He's <u>really</u> cute.

SPANISH DIARY

JULIA SCHEERES

JULIA SCHEERES is the author of the *New York Times* and *London Times* bestselling memoir *Jesus Land*. Her second book, *A Thousand Lives: The Untold Story of Jonestown*, was named the Best Nonfiction Book of 2012 by the Northern California Booksellers Association, and a best book of the year by the *San Francisco Chronicle* and the *Boston Globe*. She's published creative nonfiction in the *New York Times*, *Wired*, *San Francisco Chronicle*, and the *Guardian*, and taught narrative nonfiction in San José State University's MFA program. She is a frequent contributor to the *New York Times Book Review*.

I regret everything about this—that these events happened, that I wrote them down, that they're being published in this book. I was in my early twenties when I wrote these diary entries, trying to figure out the meaning of life. Reading them now, their nonsensical earnestness—their grasping at profundity—makes my ears cringe.

I kept this diary after moving to Valencia, Spain, where I'd fallen in love with a tall, ravishingly sexy antiterrorist agent named Serafin. We moved into a flat in the old part of town and lived a charmed life . . . and Serafin became more and more controlling. I left him many times, but hot sex always lured me back. (He gave me my first orgasm—I don't regret that!) We fought, we fucked.

We fought, we fucked. Such was the rhythm of our relationship. But then he grew paranoid. He thought I was screwing my boss and that his colleagues were plotting against him. Fed up, I returned to the States. He called me every night. He told me he was in therapy. He asked me to marry him, and I said yes. I loved him. I flew back to Spain to find him in a mental hospital outside of Madrid, and the doctors released him into my care. Then things got really interesting. . . .

—J.S.

Scheeres's portrait of Serafin. Translation: "Do you remember the day we made love under the olive tree in Sevilla? It was so hot and when the farmer passed on his tractor we laughed and you covered me with your body."

The Surging Violence

The urge to hurt Serafin is dominant. The impulse to bludgeon him rather than caress him, is predominant. On his 27th birthday, I gave him a bloody lip. It felt soooo good to materialize a year's bitterness, to serve 3 good blows to his face.

Situation: went to El Palmar for paella. Good meal, light conversation. He goes to pay bill, I to the toilet. When I come out, shades of darkness creep across his face. Here we go again. In the car he says, "I can't stand this any more. I want you to return to the flat. You belong there."

Me: "No."

"Then get your stuff out. I want to bring women over."

"You can fuck whoever you want."

He backtracks. I don't remember the words, but yes, the screeching voice. I open the door (going down the highway). He grabs my wrists in a vise-grip. I peel off his fingers and I hit him full-force in the face, 3 times. Relief. He cries, saying, "Hit me. But don't leave me."

4/5/91

Thought: I'll never really be able to love a man because they have been mentalized too long, too thoroughly, in a way which goes against the very essence of my morals in oppressing women. I'll never find a man capable of throwing his shit of the privileged sex aside and see me for what I am: above all a human.

No, I'm not a woman. I'm a human. I'm a being inside a feminine body. Unfortunately, men see only surface elements. I'm neither woman, nor race, nor sex. I'm me. Julia Kay Scheeres. Always.

Contemplating the entropy of a sick society. The man of my dreams, that restless feminist whom I could love without boundaries: where is he?

10/24/91

Today I walked the streets feeling openly sensual. Totally femme fatale. Confident, sexy, yet despising the male race. It showed. My aloof horniness was greeted with numerous compliments. I wouldn't mind having another affair. With Serafin gone, I feel more vibrant, more alive, aware of my surroundings and OPEN to them. Anything can happen—ya veremos (we'll see).

9/1/1992

The world is new, plastic, artificial and unable to transform into more than flesh and filth. There is no nobility, dignity, purity, pure love. When will we be able to marvel at the simple treasures life has to offer us without littering the scenery with our cheap egotistical caprices? Is that what really matters?

FAMILY FARMACY POEMS

JEFF GREENWALD is also the title in the splatter graphic: JEFF GREENWALD

JEFF GREENWALD's books include *Shopping for Buddhas, The Size of the World* (for which he created the first Internet travel blog), and *Snake Lake*. His far-flung voyages, fraught with odd illuminations and social blunders, have provided rich material for his storytelling career. Greenwald's acclaimed one-man show, *Strange Travel Suggestions*, premiered in San Francisco in 2003. He is also the executive director of EthicalTraveler.org, a nonprofit alliance dedicated to human rights and environmental protection.

In 1974, when I moved to San Francisco from New York, there was a popular café on California Street called the Family Farmacy. Every Monday night, during the all-you-can-eat spaghetti feed, I read my poetry with great conviction to the annoyed clientele of the Farmacy. Eventually, I browbeat the owner of this doomed establishment into publishing a slim volume of my work. The book was titled *Amber Fortress*. I thought of my soul as a struggling creature that, like some unfortunate insects of the Mesozoic, would be preserved for eternity in the hardened sap of those poems.

The following year, I enrolled at UC Santa Cruz, pursuing a degree in psychology. But the role of tortured artist is difficult to shed, and poetry remained a strong focus. The bacchanal of college life provided yet another agar for purple verse.

Reading back over these poems today, it seems they share a theme of love-torn angst—the overarching mind-set of my twenties. I wish I could say they embarrass me, but I sort of envy that obsessive young writer. He threw himself into matters of the heart so urgently, so shamelessly. But much of him is still familiar to me, after all these years. I may have shed my illusions about the mystical power of washing machines, but I never outgrew my fascination with marine mammals.

—J.G.

5

jeff greenwald
4-75 SF
1:00

TUESDAY NIGHT

I ran alone through the tube grass
in the dusk, toward the gray and purple
distance of sky and Pacific joining
in a pact of fog;
and I first thought there were others,
from the sound of a nearby transistor radio...
But I couldn't make out the songs, there were
no real words, and breaking away from the moment's
stoned blank haze I realized:
There is no radio.
The seals are singing
to the vanishing evening, barking through a pain
I could never understand,
going back a thousand years....
to a beach free of lights, bridges,
concrete walls and tourist traps.
I stood on a cliff,
facing the Ocean/and the seals,
and sang one note:
In my cracking voice, one note shouted
at the lights and tar.
And the seals stopped singing to listen.
I could imagine them turning to face me
in the dark.

Jeff Greenwald
10-20-76

...it all comes off in the wash

The morning after you left,
I walked around the room -
couldn't figure out what was wrong.
I picked some of the books up,
cleaned off the desk,
forced the drawers shut -
still no good.
I sat down on the bed to think it over,
and sprang to my feet...
Of course!
THE SHEETS!
I husked the bed bare;
yanked off the soiled white sheets
and stuffed them into a pillowcase.
My hand shied back - yaaaaaaaah! -
from the stains and blood stains
and stains which almost seemed damp.
Without hesitation I stuffed these sheets deep the washer
into the washer; added too much detergent,
Hot wash, Hot rinse,
sat on the washer as it spun,
spun furiously,
All of you off my sheets,
Every night, off my sheets,
All those stains spinning
Off me and my sheets.

TEN MINUTES TO MIDNIGHT

JULIA SCOTT

JULIA SCOTT is a radio producer, journalist, and essayist based in San Francisco. Her work has been collected in *The Best American Science Writing*. Her stories have appeared in the *New York Times Magazine*, *Modern Farmer*, *Nautilus*, *Salon*, and on PRI's Marketplace and the BBC World Service. Oh, yeah, she also edited this book. No regrets there. She just wishes you weren't about to read on.

///

At ten minutes to midnight on October 26, 2000, I walked out on the balcony of my dorm room in Paris with a notebook. I was living in Paris for my junior year abroad, and I remember the streets were quiet and dark—the perfect setting for what was to come.

In ten minutes, I would turn twenty—a birthday I had been waiting for for so long that the moment itself felt too momentous to ignore. (I was also in the midst of a full-blown existential crisis—very Parisian—and had been awake, tossing and turning, on each dark night that year.) So feel free to picture me as I was that night, a virginal nineteen-year-old in a flannel nightgown, alone and shivering on a balcony with a notebook and facing the last night of her teenage years. Here is what I wrote.

—J.S.

10/26/00
11:50 p.m.

I am about to write a paragraph of HYPOCRISY,
because although I am about to write that I attach no
significance whatsoever to my 20th birthday, this is
belied by the fact that I am desperately writing about
it in the last moment of my "adolescence."

But it's true—I could care less about my birthday.
Birthdays themselves are as arbitrary as the dates and
hours that were invented to hold time in the hot hand
of humanity.

The number "20" is as meaningless as the hour I
fixed at the top of this entry. And any significance
I attach to it is socially constructed. This fact was
reinforced by the sudden realization, while standing by
the window and waiting for midnight to arrive, that my
birthday had already begun in North America!

If I MUST attach any significance to an artificial
number that indicates neither a "phase" nor a
"milestone," I would say that, taking it at face value,
it indicates a new set of experiences to be had. To
use the term "the twenties"—the twenties have GOT to be
better than the "teens." That is why I am happy to age,
to definitively (at least from the point of view of
OTHERS who attach importance to "20"), say that those
years are behind me.

Why not use "20" as a jumping-off point for a
happier, healthier Julia?

At the same time, in contemplating the fact that
I have been on this earth for twenty human years, I

become unbelievably hopeless. Twenty years, within the course of nature's history, is dust. It's dust on dust.

It's atoms on dust on dust.

And yet, for my "20" years, I feel as though I haven't yet read enough, haven't thought or felt enough. I should have a chef d'oeuvre to show for it by now, shouldn't I, or at least be very, very wise?

I feel like I'm not SEEING enough. Where are the moments of absolute suffering and joy that complement each other in a cycle of happiness and pain, love and hate?

I want to experience LIFE viscerally, but at the same time step back and think about it all. Most of all, I'm afraid that in the coming years all my midnight scribblings will come to nothing, and are just the self-centered scratches of someone who knows of no other way to lend significance to her life.

4

ODDITIES

It tastes like apples; crunchy and mushy / That's the first time that I ate a pussy.

—Nathaniel Rich

2 DEAD MOO: AS SICK AND PERVERTED AS THEY WANNA BE

NATHANIEL RICH

NATHANIEL RICH is the author of two novels, *Odds Against Tomorrow* and *The Mayor's Tongue*. His essays appear regularly in the *New York Review of Books*, *Harper's*, *Rolling Stone*, and the *New York Times Magazine*. He lives in New Orleans.

Nathaniel Rich and his friend Charley.

My grandfather's generation had Glenn Miller; my father had John Lennon. I had Luke Skyywalker. Not the character from *Star Wars*—the Miami rapper best known as the frontman for the 2 Live Crew. In 1989, the year that *As Nasty As They Wanna Be* was released, I did not know what "Put Her in the Buck" meant, but that song, along with such chestnuts as "My Seven Bizzos," "Bad Ass Bitch," "The Fuck Shop," and the single that elevated 2 Live Crew to national notoriety and double-platinum record sales, "Me So Horny," mesmerized me. Those songs, and their lyrics, were unlike anything I had ever heard before. In retrospect this is not particularly surprising because at the time I'd just turned nine years old.

My parents did not allow me to buy the album. I had to settle instead for the bowdlerized version, *As Clean As They Wanna Be*. (A sample lyric change: "Sitting at home with my dick on hard" became "Sitting at home watching Arsenio Hall.") But my friend Charley Stern—who that year had become something of a celebrity at our elementary school for appearing on *Reading Rainbow*, where he recommend Ezra Jack Keats's *The Snowy Day*, a picture book about a boy named Peter who makes a snowman—had somehow obtained a samizdat copy of the explicit version. Charley brought it to school one day, hidden in a Yanni case. We were good kids, angelically behaved, adoring of our mothers and teachers, and just the act of staring at the cassette—in the boys' bathroom, the door locked—felt illicit, forbidden, and more than a little dangerous. We pledged to listen to the album together, in its entirety. We asked our parents to arrange a sleepover at his house for the coming Friday night. When the day finally arrived, we locked ourselves in his bedroom and listened to the album straight through six times in a row in the closest thing to a narcotized daze that is possible for a pair of nine-year-olds.

Over dinner, in a fit of inspiration and giddiness, we had a revelation. We would make a tribute album. Charley had everything we'd need: a Casio synthesizer that could loop keyboard and beats; a Playskool turntable and an EPMD album that we would scratch during rap breaks; a blank cassette; a tape recorder. We called ourselves the 2 Dead Moo.

We spent about six hours writing the music and lyrics for sixteen songs, in which we tried, to the best of our abilities, to match the porno-crazed deviance of the Crew. (There was one exception: our song "Me So Boring" was more satire than emulation; it was about a guy who, instead of picking up girls at strip clubs and having sex with them like Luke Skyywalker, stayed at home and ate peanut butter sandwiches.) As nine-year-olds who had never imagined trying to kiss a girl, we knew it would not be easy to outdo lines like "She'll climb a mount, even run the block / Just to kiss the head of this big black cock" (from "Dick Almighty"); or the frenzied call-and-response of "Do You Believe in Having Sex?" ("All the ladies say, 'Eat this pussy, eat-eat this puss-say.'") But we'd try.

We didn't sleep that night; it was the most feverishly creative twenty-four hours of my life. We practiced a song until we had it down, then we'd record it in a single take. When my mother came to pick me up the following afternoon, we had just completed the album, *As Sick and Perverted As They Wanna Be*, including liner notes and cover art. Not that I told her about it.

I'm proud to say that, twenty-five years later, the lyrics still have the power to shock—to shock my wife at least. This is why I'm withholding, for instance, the lyrics to our opening track, "Buttfuckin'."

As you read these excerpts, keep in mind that they were performed by two boys with falsetto voices. Please don't show this to my mother. Or yours.

—N.R.

OPENING SKIT:
Mother's voice: Tony, what are you listening to?
Kid: Oh, it's just the New Kids on the Block.
Mother: What sweet boys. OK, I'll leave now.
Kid: Enough of this bullshit. It's time to listen to the 2 DEAD MOO.

"We Is Who We Am"
We is who we am
And that's who we want to be
If you call us dicks, that's okay with WE

We talk about pussies
Dicks and asses, too
If you think that's crazy
We'll throw you in a zoo

"Get Funky"

When you listen to the Moo, you get busy
You dance so much that you're dizzy
You get horny after every show
You go to the whorehouse
And you get yourself a ho
You lick her tits and start to chew
And you shout out loud,
"We're the 2 Dead Moo!"

"Ain't No Sucka"

Don't try to impress me
'Cause you'll wind up having sex with me
Your pussy, it ain't good
Please don't treat it like it's wood
Oh my god, you're a hooker
Well, I ain't no sucka

Remember, I'm on the mic
And I'm the right kind of guy to
Fuck with, yeah, me and you
Hand in hand, in and out
Fuckin' all night and I'm gonna shout
Oooh, he's just a fucker
What was that?
I ain't no sucka

"Da Ho"

Oh shit
I was at a whorehouse, watching a show
DA HO

Up in my attic, looking down
I saw one horny ho in a gown
I said, "Yo, ho, come to your bro."
She said, "Fine! Is there wine?"
I said, "Yeah, we can dine."
She came up and had a 7UP
And then—she threw up
Even when she was sick, she really could go
Then she left and now I miss . . . DA HO

She sucks a good dick!

"How to Eat a Pussy"
A little bit of trouble, but it's worth the wait
When she comes, it will go all over your face
The first time I did it, I was 29
The girl really liked it and so did I
It tastes like apples; crunchy and mushy
That's the first time that I ate a pussy

CHUCK PALAHNIUK

DEAR MR. POL POT

CHUCK PALAHNIUK is the bestselling author of *Fight Club*, *Choke*, and a dozen other books, the most recent of which are *Doomed* and *Beautiful You*. In 1975, his younger sister, Heidi, became a celebrity at Columbia Middle School in Burbank, Washington, when she received a tersely worded letter from the Pinochet government, banning her from ever entering Chile.

In 1972, when I was ten years old and my sister, Heidi, was nine, we both joined Amnesty International.

Each month the group sent us a newsletter describing then current human rights violations, focusing mainly on the people being tortured as political prisoners. The newsletter also gave the names and mailing addresses of their captors and encouraged us to write in protest. It was the golden age of the letter-writing campaign.

Our family had a typewriter our mother had bought in the 1950s and used so sparingly that it still had its original ribbon. We also owned a complete set of the *World Book Encyclopedia*, which was chockablock with fancy-pants words, useful facts, slightly out-of-date movie star photographs, and maps. A few of them printed in color! Aleksandr Solzhenitsyn was the last political detainee to register on our mother's radar, and since he'd won the Nobel Prize in 1970, she encouraged us to write in pencil like her hero. Besides, typewriter ribbons were too costly for kids to waste. My sister took it a step further and wrote in purple crayon. Heidi wrote as a nine-year-old girl in fourth grade, attempting to shame whatever dictator with her child's superior sense of morality.

I, on the other hand, knew the truth: coldhearted fascists couldn't be shamed.

I was in fifth grade and was well acquainted with bullies. "Baby Doc" Duvalier, Augusto Pinochet, Francisco Franco, or Mobutu Sese Seko would only laugh coldly while reading my little sister's erstwhile plea and then sip a refreshing draught of human blood out of a cup fashioned from a skull before immediately going back to lashing some trussed-up, half-naked ideological opponent.

This was the 1970s, the era of détente, but wily diplomacy and clever statecraft could only get a person so far with pen pals like Nicolae Ceauşescu. The sole thing bullies understood was power. This was my chance to be a letter-writing James Bond. The number two pencil was mightier than the sword. What follows is typical of the arm-twisting correspondence I fired off to cutthroat despots around the world.

—C.P.

Dear Mr. Pol Pot,

Perhaps you'll recall our last meeting, perhaps not. Wistfully, I trust you do. It was many years ago lounging on the rooftop terrace of the Hotel Le Royal in the fashionable heart of Phnom Penh, a city of so many, many charms. There, among a distinguished crowd of international jetsetters, we raised our glasses to the sunset over the Mekong River, and you delivered a hilarious bon mot comparing the rapturous eventide spectacle to Henry Kissinger's rather louche eyewear.

For many years, your rapier wit has held a special place in my memory.

Alas, imagine my dismay upon hearing from Amnesty International that you've been conducting a wholesale slaughter of your own innocent citizens. To say how deeply I'm disappointed in you . . . well, words fail me.

Fully known to you is that fact that I'm a billionaire industrialist with my fingers in many a lucrative pie. I'd be remiss if I didn't mention my plans to build a humongous manufacturing plant in your country, bringing boatloads of American dollars into your fragile, struggling economy. But, on second thought, investing capital in a nation that neglects basic human rights seems a tad unwise. Your actions compel me to rethink the option of sitting my state-of-the-art eight-track-tape assembly line in a more peasant-friendly environ.

Until this matter of the butchered multitudes is cleared up to my satisfaction, please consider my factory-building plans to be on hold.

Oh that this were my only change-of-heart.

Strictly as a divertissement, I also produce big-budget Hollywood epics, and it had long been my dream to remake "From Here to Eternity" on location in your lovely semitropical clime. No less an actress than Gina Lollobrigida was set to play the female lead. Needless to say, Gina is heartsick to hear of your genocidal preoccupations for she has harbored a fantasy of making your acquaintance and indulging you with her world-renown qualities.

And while it was not my original intention to dangle the luscious Jill St. John like an enticing bauble just beyond your reach, she has also secretly craved an introduction. That said, you must realize that these western beauties will not think highly of a man, even a virile, charismatic world leader, who turns perfectly good rice paddies into killing fields. Being a gentleman, I'm not at liberty to divulge the glorious sexual favors such ladies can bestow. Suffice to say that you staging large-scale pogroms hardly acts as Spanish fly upon the comely likes of Ursula Andress and Linda Evans.

If you'll permit me to say, we're both gentlemen of the world. Let's call a bribe by its proper name. If you can see your way to sparing future victims, I could make certain delightful assignations possible. Pharmaceutical-grade "party favors," included. Wink-wink.

As for myself, personally, I prefer to recall you as the jovial, Kissinger-baiting goofball. Judging character is my forte. It saddens me to discover I could be so mistaken. If you have anything to say in your own defense, please do not hesitate to ring me up. At present I reside at the Viceroy Hotel in Mozambique. I am registered under the name Latimer Keegan for purposes of privacy while outlining additional film projects with Ms. Lollobrigida and Ms. St. John.

P.S. You might also be receiving an indignant missive from someone named Heidi Jeanette Palahniuk, who claims to be my younger sister. Please do not take what she says lightly. It's not without good reason that she writes like a moron. Neither is she, as she claims, a lithe young fourth-grader. She is in fact my deranged older sibling. A thyroid condition has rendered her the size of a Silverback gorilla, and she boasts the physical strength of ten men. Like me, she was very dismayed by the tip-off from Amnesty International. Please be on the constant lookout for her for she will not hesitate to savagely rend you limb from limb.

Ciao bello,
Charles Palahniuk

JUGGLING JAKE

AMY TAN's novels are *The Joy Luck Club*, *The Kitchen God's Wife*, *The Hundred Secret Senses*, *The Bonesetter's Daughter*, and *Saving Fish from Drowning*, all *New York Times* bestsellers and recipients of various awards. She is also the author of a memoir, *The Opposite of Fate*; two children's books, *The Moon Lady* and *Sagwa, The Chinese Siamese Cat*; and numerous articles for magazines, including the *New Yorker*, *Harper's Bazaar*, and *National Geographic*. She is also the author of the short story "Rules for Virgins," published in ebook format (Byliner Originals). Her work has been translated into thirty-five languages. Her most recent novel is *The Valley of Amazement.*

//

Boy, was I good at rhyming. It helped that my grammar was bad ("pieces" —> "it") and sometimes archaic ("And down they did come and did break") and that there happened to be a town named Hoodit. Juggling Jake is still in the slammer in the Hoodit county jail for selling damaged goods on eBay.

—A.T.

A JUGGLER NAMED JAKE

There was a juggler named Jake,
Who everyone called a fake.
He tossed in the air,
Plates by the pair.
And down they did come and did break.

He went to a town called "Hoodit."
And there he learned how to do it.
Not toss up the plates,
That he did break
But take the pieces and glue it.

by Amy Tan

A. J. JACOBS

TWO FEGHOOTS
(AFTER PYNCHON)

A. J. JACOBS is the author of the *New York Times* bestsellers *The Know-It-All*, *The Year of Living Biblically*, and *The Guinea Pig Diaries*. He is the editor at large of *Esquire* magazine, a contributor to NPR, and has written for the *New York Times*, *Washington Post*, and *Entertainment Weekly*. He lives in New York City with his wife and their kids. Visit him at AJJacobs.com.

Jacobs and his mom.

//

Here's an embarrassing little chapter of my writing life. When I was twenty-two, I tried to emulate Thomas Pynchon. The results were not pretty.

In *Gravity's Rainbow*, Pynchon goes on a weird ten-page detour that tells the story of dwarves (as he put it) who stole fur coats, then auditioned to be in a biblical epic directed by Cecille B. DeMille. They wanted to play slaves on a galleon. DeMille rejected them.

Pynchon ends the story with the sentence: "For De Mille young fur-henchmen can't be rowing." Which turns out to be an elaborate pun on the phrase "Forty million Frenchmen can't be wrong."

I don't even like puns very much, but I thought Pynchon was so darn clever, I wanted to try to craft my own stories that ended in excruciating puns. (I've since found out this an actual genre of literature called the Feghoot.)

My Feghoot attempts were so bad, I have kept them safely in my hard drive for years. Here are two. The first one isn't just bad, it's culturally offensive.

—A.J.J.

1.

I met a man from Kentucky. He told me "Ya know, ah often go flyin' with mah wife, mah nephew and mah niece. But mah wife, she gits turned on when she's up in the air, so as soon as we take off, she and mah nephew go to the back of the plane to do some hanky panky.

So I asked him, "Do you do stay in the front of the plane to do some hanky panky as well."

To which he replied, "No. Mah niece and I land."

[No man is an island]

2.

Fanny was off to the market. But before she went, she asked her husband, Clive, for some money.

OK, said Clive, as he gave her three pounds. "But I'm very short, so I need whatever change you get back."

Fanny came back with a big sirloin steak and a bottle of scotch. How much change did you get, asked Clive.

Only twopence, said Fanny. "But something's been bothering me all the way home. The checkout girl had a big hairdo that stuck way up to the ceiling. I know there's a name for that hairdo. I know there's a word for it. What's the word, Clive?"

"The pence, my dear. Then this word."

[The pen is mightier than the sword]

CHRIS COLIN

MY WIFE MOVED TO CHILE

CHRIS COLIN is the author most recently of *What to Talk About*, as well as *What Really Happened to the Class of '93* and *Blindsight*, named one of Amazon's Best Books of 2011. He's written about chimp filmmakers, ethnic cleansing, George Bush's pool boy, blind visual artists, solitary confinement, the Yelpification of the universe, and more for NewYorker.com, the *New York Times Magazine*, the *Atavist*, *Outside*, *Wired*, *Smithsonian*, *Mother Jones*, *McSweeney's*, and *Afar*, where he's a contributing writer. He lives in San Francisco with his wife and kids.

Poetry is a lonely slog. Its practitioners toil in obscurity for years, and only a fraction ever publish, usually in some equally obscure local journal.

Other poets, I'm talking about. Me, the first poem I ever wrote won a prestigious contest and was published in a prominent anthology. I was twenty-two. Like Whitman and Dickinson before me, I drew from a deep well of fascinating feelings, plus used the tab button a bunch to make the poetry that much better. The highest quality is essential if you're writing about how your girlfriend, whom you call your wife to sound more significant, goes to South America for a while.

The rules of the poetry industry surprised me. Instead of paying, this anthology charged me $50. And when it arrived, the address seemed scrawled by a child. It was bound, in the sense that your fifth-grade report on sharks was bound.

Some might say I fell for a moronic scam, and paid for the publication of the only poem I ever wrote. Wordy! Quicker just to say I'm a published poet.

—C.C.

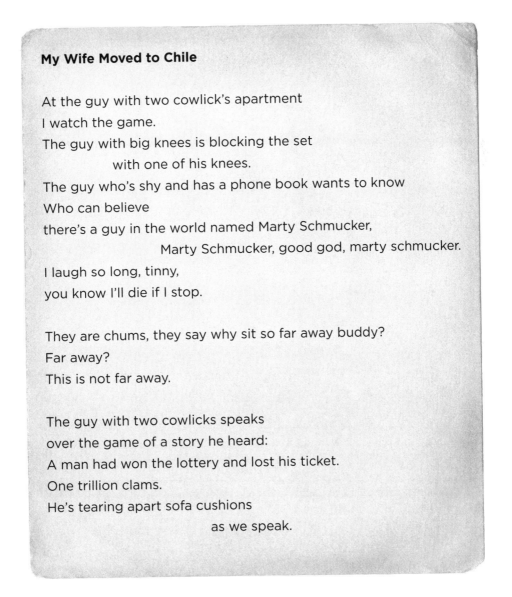

My Wife Moved to Chile

At the guy with two cowlick's apartment
I watch the game.
The guy with big knees is blocking the set
       with one of his knees.
The guy who's shy and has a phone book wants to know
Who can believe
there's a guy in the world named Marty Schmucker,
          Marty Schmucker, good god, marty schmucker.
I laugh so long, tinny,
you know I'll die if I stop.

They are chums, they say why sit so far away buddy?
Far away?
This is not far away.

The guy with two cowlicks speaks
over the game of a story he heard:
A man had won the lottery and lost his ticket.
One trillion clams.
He's tearing apart sofa cushions
        as we speak.

DEAR MR. NIXON

CAROLINE PAUL is the author of a memoir, *Fighting Fire*, and a novel, *East Wind, Rain*. Her most recent book, *Lost Cat: A True Story of Love, Desperation, and GPS Technology*, with drawings by Wendy MacNaughton, was published in 2013.

The year is 1973. President Nixon has just been reelected to a second term, the United States is still embroiled in Vietnam, Deep Throat has begun speaking to the *Washington Post*, and now Congress in investigating what will soon be the Watergate scandal.

We are on the cusp of an oil embargo and a stock market crash. Clearly we are a country disillusioned with our government and losing faith by the day.

But as you can tell, I was someone who believed in authority. I had concerns, and this was America—and so I decided to write a letter to President Richard Nixon. And he replied. I was nine years old.

—C.P.

Dear Mr. Nixon,

I am glad you won. We still get the magizines from New York. Can you send me your autograph?

I am going to tell you a knock-knock joke.

Knock-knock!

Who is there?

Warren

Warren who?

Warren Peace by Leo Tolstoy.

Will you please do something to help stop pollution in New York. Also will you help people in need? You should see how mistreated animals are! Horses are whipped, not with crops, with whips! Cats and Dogs are mistreated and not well fed. Then when the owners get tired of thier animals they kick them out of the house instead of giving them to the A.S.P.C.A!

Later, the animals die from lack of food and shelter. Sometimes, before the animals die, they give birth and then either die or leave their babies on thier own and then they die. Sometimes the babies grow up to be alley cats and then there are so many animals that are stray that you must kill them! Some people keep animals in the city and then the animals go mad for the out side and soon die.

This must stop! If you don't watch out the animals may soon over populate and what can you do? How can you stop and catch the animals to stop them having babies? You can't I don't think!

Caroline Paul
(and sister Alexandra)

THE WHITE HOUSE

WASHINGTON

April 18, 1973

Dear Caroline and Alexandra:

No matter how busy my day is, I am
always pleased to hear from boys and
girls who take the time to write and
share their thoughts about America
with me. Your comments concerning
cruelty to animals tell me that you
care very much about helping those
who cannot help themselves, and you
should always cherish this sensitivity.

The example you set by your concern
for God's creatures with whom we
share this earth can be your first
step toward helping to build a better
world for animals -- and for people.
Keep up the good work!

With my best wishes for the years
ahead,

Sincerely,

Richard Nixon

Miss Caroline Paul
Miss Alexandra Paul
30 Villa Dupont
Paris 16
France

THE ARMOIRE

TUPELO HASSMAN

TUPELO HASSMAN's first novel, *Girlchild*, was published by Farrar, Straus and Giroux. Her work has appeared in the *Boston Globe*, *Harper's Bazaar*, *Imaginary Oklahoma*, the *Independent UK*, the *Paris Review Daily*, the *Portland Review Literary Journal*, *sPARKLE & bLINK*, and *ZYZZYVA*, and has been published by 100WordStory .org, FiveChapters.com, and Invisible City Audio Tours, among others. More is forthcoming from *Girls on Fire: Stories of and for Teen Girls*. Hassman is the first American to win London's Literary Death Match. She lives in San Francisco's East Bay where she can often be found having a root beer on tap at the Hog's Apothecary.

///

It's always an old man. He comes out of the bathroom, "Pssst." He's tantalizing in the way of old men, the kind who wear one-piece worksuits that zip from neck to balls. You're not waiting fifty years for the kind of wisdom that lets you get away with wearing what is basically a grown-up onesie. You're ready for enlightenment now, and so you come closer and he tells you this, "You got to see the shit I just took. Long as my arm!"

If you can imagine me in one of those old-man crazy suits, which I have been known to wear, you're ready to read this piece. And I do mean "piece." My writing here is like that old man's shit. Except that I am less proud of it. And except that the first person to peek at it was Vicki Forman, my creative writing prof at the time I pen-pooped it. Poor Vicki. Poor you.

When I was asked to be a part of *Drivel*, I figured I'd hand over a story I'd never finalized, an unpolished but still hopeful work, something to make readers say, "Well, that Tupelo Hassman, she can't write a bad word if she tries." I'd call out the faults of the submission, winking all the while at how there's still gold in them thar hills, but that, seeing as how this is for Litquake and all, for a good cause, like a philanthropic prostitute, I'm willing to show my knickers.

But this piece has me in less than knickers. I'm naked here. Under fluorescent lights. After a bad night. An old man's crazy suit around my ankles. Pssst.

—T.H.

When they split she had to move to a studio apartment with no closet. She hated it, the apartment, the move, the break up. She could afford neither, and neither could she afford the armoire but more costly was the feeling of having been defeated which was made more pronounced by the piles of clothes that surrounded her bed.

The armoire cost $400, delivery included, and was her first piece of furniture. Everything else was handed down or found on the sidewalks or in alleys on trash days. It had a full-length mirror and a closet, not shelves, on the inside. These were her only qualifications and it was the only one she found that matched them.

She was proud of it. Maybe too proud, and when he returned (as he always did) and before they could have one conversation she was sitting on the upholstered lining of the armoire's closet floor, legs out, head resting on her winter coats as he marked the piece of furniture with their reunion.

THE ROUNDABOUT STORY OF CAPTAIN TORITO

KIERA BUTLER, a senior editor at *Mother Jones*, lives in Oakland, California. Having already penned the definitive work on Captain Torito, she switched gears and is currently working on her first book, *Raise: What 4-H Teaches 7 Million Kids—and How Its Lessons Could Change Food and Farming Forever* (forthcoming in late 2014).

///

The strange thing about this story is that I have no memory of ever being interested in anything maritime when I wrote this during Mrs. Sullivan's fifth-grade class (I was ten). My guess is that I had either recently gone on a whale watch or just finished Joan Aiken's great book *Nightbirds on Nantucket*, which I remember being sort of swashbuckling.

In general, as a kid I was much more into landlubbing stories such as the *Little House on the Prairie* books and *Caddie Woodlawn*. At any rate, I think I got bored about halfway through writing this story, hence the cursory treatment of the many dangers that befell the captain, "such as cannibals." Also, I think I named the captain after Doritos.

—K.B.

Being a captain on the world famous ship, Santa Rosita, I have stumbled upon many a strange phenomenon. 'Tis why I decided to put the story of one of my adventures in writing. My name is Captain Torito. I come from Spain. Most of my journeys are to the Spice Islands. After the Turks took over Constantinople, it made it quite difficult to get from Spain to the Spice Islands, and back. However, I earned my living doing map work and other things of the sort, so I muddled through. And here my story begins; let it put knowledge of the demon the sea into your mind.

'Twas a right down windy day in the month of March. My crew and I were returning from the Spice Islands. I was mapping out a way to get back. "Hark!" I said. I had found the perfect route! I will explain it to you, my beloved reader, now.

I was to sail west of the Indies, until I came to the southern tip of India. I would sail around it, and then across the Indian Ocean to the Red Sea. I would then go north, until I came to a spot of land before the Mediterranean Sea. Then I would leave the boat at the spot of land, with guards. (Thieves, you know!) Then I would rent horses to take us to the Med. Sea. When we got to the Med. Sea, I would hire a boat to sail to Genoa!

So we sailed our route, running into many dangers, such as Cannibals, on the tip of India, and Turks near the Med. Sea.

However we did make it back to Genoa, with only one life lost. I got paid a rather large sum of money for my journey.

This concludes my story. I hope you thoroughly enjoyed it.

COWBOY UP

ANDREW SEAN GREER

ANDREW SEAN GREER is the bestselling author of five works of fiction, most recently *The Impossible Lives of Greta Wells*. He is the recipient of the Northern California Book Award, the California Book Award, the NYPL Young Lions Award, and fellowships from the NEA and the New York Public Library. He once dated a cowboy.

Greer at the age of twenty-five with fellow MFA student Mary Park, who is still friends with him despite his early bad writing.

When I graduated from the University of Montana with my MFA, I had a few thousand dollars left over from my student grants, and I decided I would live on this money while I wrote a new novel. That gave me about four months, which seemed like a reasonable amount of time. I was twenty-five. I was living with my new boyfriend in Seattle, in a house that looked out on downtown and the Cascade mountain range and whose rent was cheap because we had to take care of the owner's Siamese cat, Vrtiska, who would only be silent when she sat on my lap. My boyfriend traveled constantly. I had no money to eat anything but tuna salad, and so did Vrtiska. And so, with the arrogance and passion of youth, I dashed off a novel about thieves who counterfeit cowboy art, and a car chase across the West.

I wrote eight pages a day, every day. It was called *Cowboy Up* or *Fascinatin' Tim*. Fascinatin' Tim was the villain. I believe the climax was at a geyser or a ghost town or something—I have not reread it in nearly twenty years. I sent it off to my agent, very proud. And he never mentioned it to me except once, years later, when he said he kept it in his bedside table as a reminder of where we all came from.

I abandoned the novel—I married the boyfriend. But I have to say, reading over the beginning of that novel, it has the charm of an old high school yearbook photo. Ugly and awkward and unlovable. But what a naive smile it wears on its face!

—A.S.G.

True story:

It was a costume dance to benefit the Olympic mountain range, but by some amazing coincidence, all the young women had come dressed as Spanish ladies. So then picture it: almost a hundred red silk skirts spidered with black lace, dancing across the room like toppled poison mushrooms, whole galaxies of beauty spots glimmering from frowning cheeks, countless rose-stenciled fans flapping away at furious female breasts, causing a sound like sprinklers on a college lawn as well as, more strikingly, near gale-force winds which lifted every one of a hundred mantillas straight into the air. The effect: an Old West bordello reunion. The mood: bitter feminine fury.

So how would you expect the men to act? First, we could hardly believe our good luck. The first sight was an impressive mountain chain of cleavage—"Alps on Alps" as Pope (I think) once put it. But shock soon followed. We men, dressed as bumblebees, fringed cowboys, fleeting political celebrities and appliances, couldn't tell one from the other. That sounds offensive. I don't mean to sound offensive; I mean to flatter. Sometimes when I talk about women, some of my twin brother Galen flashes through and I sound bug-eyed and lecherous. So please imagine the dance floor of the Seattle Brotherhood of Benevolent Antelope blooming with these Spanish poppies and you'll see my totally male confusion. To have two women look alike is one thing (I've learned, from being a twin, that women think this about men, too). To have all possible women look alike is a dreary fantasy.

I'm really not used to talking about me. All the stories I've ever told have been about my twin brother Galen, whose life has been far more exciting than mine. Most of our years between puberty and that costume ball were spent together talking about his life, whispering and laughing, me always wide-eyed at his stories of seduction, him always leaning back into a chair and beginning, "Here's our lesson for the day. . . ." He told me the tricks to his seductions. I learned how to dress to provoke, the precise aperture of a bewitching eye, the language of roses, love letters, wax seals and how to pine with perfection.

He taught me what to think about love, how it felt, what one should be willing to do for it, and when he suddenly fled Seattle a month before this costume ball, my world changed, lost depth; I was a man without a sense of smell. Without his bright arrogance, I had only stretches of long gray days, but I learned not to judge them on their length, their grayness or their same cloth patterns in the sky.

So I stood alone on that dance floor at the costume party, dressed as only half a pantomime ox (the latter half, if you have to know), blinded intermittently by the blue reflections of the mirror ball, the strobes, the flashing jewelry, staring at the gaggles of Donna Annas lifting their skirts trying to win a dance.

And I tried not to be me. I closed my eyes and tried to remember what he'd taught me, how to charm a person into your life. I missed him, and tried to be him.

I was making a little progress in the corner, behind the taxidermy diorama of an antelope outstripping a wolf. The lady I was talking with had the same costume as all the others, but after my eyes adjusted to the light and I saw through her veil, I could tell she had small, careful eyes and a face the shape of a strawberry. My mother always said that

face-shape says everything about a person. Strawberries, she told me once, were the most susceptible to flattery.

"What a lovely costume," I said.

She smiled and put the rose fan to her lips. Her blond hair was curled over and over itself along her forehead so that she looked nineteenth century, some kind of grown-up Little Woman, which made her seem so lovely to me. In period costume, this was all so much easier. Her fan was at her lips and unfolded to reveal beds of red and white roses and a small rip in the fabric. She snapped it closed again and I saw her lips readying a glossy question.

"You're not Galen Darling, are you?"

A strange moment. I'll never be able to describe it to you unless you've been a twin. To be called by your twin's name isn't at all like being mistaken. Your reaction is not "That isn't me" but rather "You're seeing the wrong side."

Add to that how handsome my brother was, how he could move beyond our common genetics and outstrip me in any mirror, in any admirer's gaze. And, of course, his wickedness. I wondered for a moment if this lady knew that he was gay. I took a bold approach.

"No," I said. "I'm his twin. He's in Montana with his boyfriend." In many senses a lie, a made-up thing, and I was so terrible with lies. Perhaps I even blushed. The lady's expression, though, didn't change. Instead, she made my heart ache by smiling and (perhaps this is the imagination of memory) heaving a sigh which made her dress shift just slightly down on her breast. There were little freckles on the white skin there, and I had an urge to bob for them like apples.

She said, "I thought so. You're Johnny Darling."

"Johnny Caesar Cicero Darling," I said, raising myself proudly.

"I've been dying to talk to you," and these words came from low in her throat as she dipped forward and only a glint of green eye flashed under her mascara.

They say the corner lobes of our brains stand ready for telepathy. My mother (who knows such things) has been feeling and examining our heads (I mean mine and my twin brother Galen's) almost all our lives.

She says that his telepathic lobes are smaller than mine, but mine are completely out of use, whereas he has sparked his to near-full power. So imagine these two lobes of mine, sitting benignly beneath my skull like steel spheres of a Frankenstein generator, beginning to arc electricity between them as we two (the Spanish lady and I) stared at each other.

And I could see her eyes dilating erotically. You all know when someone's pupils dilate it means they are attracted, possibly could fall in love with you—an important clue to all be charmers. It is the eye trying to see better what it desires, and we can't control it. We also do this with chocolate. Side note: after learning this, I used to look for this dilation everywhere. For a short period, for instance, I thought everyone in my ophthalmologist's office was in love with me. When I realized it was only the eye drops, I fell into a brief depression.

5

DARK MATTER

But I am not alone now,
either. I am not alone.

—Rick Moody

WOMAN AND CLOWN

DAVE EGGERS is the author of eight books, most recently *The Circle*. Eggers is the founder and editor of McSweeney's Publishing.

DAVE EGGERS

//

I'm sorry that this is a painting, but I figured it would be a good time to shake things up in this book. And this painting is too funny to avoid.

I did this painting in high school, at the Evanston Community Center. They had classes there at night, and a portrait artist taught the class. I was among mostly older people, and everyone was very kind to me, and the teacher, whose name I can't remember but who was a burly man who painted very good and traditional portraits, could not have been nicer.

The class met at night, and every week we would have a model. For one or two weeks, the model was the woman you see in the foreground. She was nude in the traditional art-class manner, and I tried to render her faithfully. But when I was finished, I saw that I'd messed up the composition, leaving a huge negative void in the upper right.

No problem. The next week there was a different model, a man, and for some reason he was wearing clothing. Not just clothing, but some kind of clown shirt. This was the first time a model in one of the classes had worn a clown shirt.

I was sixteen, so forgive me if I thought the solution to this conundrum—unbalanced composition, man-in-clown-shirt—was to put the clown-man in the background, sitting on what would eventually look like a bed. I have no idea how I thought this would all fall together in any narrative sense. But looking at the painting now I can't believe I wasn't arrested at the time, or sent to some kind of Freudian scared-straight boot camp for would-be adolescent deviants.

—D.E.

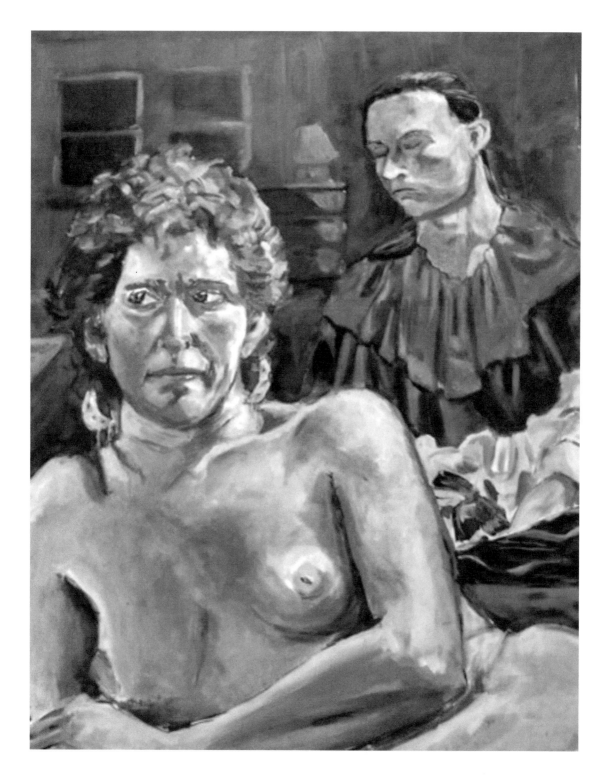

RICK
MOODY

THREE REFLECTIONS

RICK MOODY is the author of five novels, three collections of stories, a memoir, and, most recently, a collection of essays, *On Celestial Music*. He has also released two solo albums (*Rick Moody and One Ring Zero* and *The Darkness of Good*), and three albums with the Wingdale Community Singers, the latest of which is *Night, Sleep, Death*, released in 2013.

"Three Reflections" was the second story by me featured in a student publication while I was at Brown University. I am guessing that the writer of this monstrosity is twenty-one years old. The year was probably 1983. I was in a seminar with John Hawkes, in those days, which also included my friend Jeff Eugenides and several other writers who went on to produce great work.

The vibe in the Brown writing program was very experimental. For example, I'd also studied there with Robert Coover and Angela Carter, both of whom were just as uncompromising as Hawkes. (I suppose my story's patently unnecessary epigraph from Angela Carter is owing to her considerable influence on me.)

In truth, I can't tell you that much about "Three Reflections," for the simple reason that every time I attempt to reread it, I am made so depressed by its vagueness, obscurity, lack of drama, and labored voice that I want, as the kids say, to cut myself.

This refusal to reread it is apparently consistent, because if I remember correctly, the friend editing the *Issues Fiction Supplement*, in which it appeared, had to proofread the piece for me, because I couldn't bear to do it myself. That is, I refused to proofread my own story. Not a good way to begin a career.

I would tell you that I danced around the block with joy at the second appearance of my name in print, but that was not my style in those days when I was mostly busy trying to develop a full-blown drinking problem. I was probably despondent at the story's failures even then. I think the theme of the double and the mirrors in the piece (I'm reconstructing from memory!) have to do with a preoccupation with Nabokov and Borges, much on my radar then. And that is to my credit, I suppose.

To summarize, I was a mostly talentless, unfocused, self-centered student writer, who lucked into some of the best professors of the period, as well as some of the best classmates. If anything came of it, I'm sure it had mostly to do with the company I kept. Because, on the evidence of this, I don't seem to have much of a gift.

—R.M.

Three Reflections

FREDERICK MOODY

"Out of these pieces of inimical indifference I intend to represent the desolate smile of Winter which as you have gathered, is the smile I wear."

—Angela Carter

Was it the search for my twin which left me with this paralysis? It's not the twitching, numb sort—although old age has threatened to bring more of that, in knuckles and various sockets and tendons—but a different kind. It is a warm insatiable stasis, like sitting on a crowded train between two large men bent on doing harm. I am sleepy and at the same time awake. I am a jogger in place.

My twin, you see, kept turning up. This is not to be taken lightly or set aside, in the manner of my husband. It is not as he claimed that in my senility (my detractors have called it senility!) I mistook my own reflection for the fleeting image of her. On two or three occasions such a confusion took place, but philosophically speaking if this were the only possibility the locus of sightings would necessarily be the bathroom. Or the hall of mirrors, or the department store fitting room. Whichever. There has been, however, undeniable evidence of her presence in open, public places. There was none of the indecision of the bathroom sightings. There was careful observation, which may not be confused with senility.

The only solution which accounts for all possibilities is that although we separated before adulthood, by mutual agreement, my twin lived nearby the whole time, without my consent, and without my best interests at heart.

[. . .]

I remember my husband coming home as usual. He was blind, and he was bitter, and the two competed for his attentions. Dressed in his long gray tweed overcoat, he would return every afternoon at five-thirty from his job at the university for the blind. He had trouble with the doorbell out front, and so I used to meet him on the front step to help him in. If I forgot or was late, he would shout emphatically or sometimes just whack at the door with his cane though he knew well enough where the bell was.

"Miranda," he said, "I'm home." This, in the manner of all his remarks, was delivered flatly.

"I can see that," I said.

"How was your day?" he said, waiting for me to show him in. I pushed the door open and he went to the library, off the hall to the left, to sit in his armchair.

"As days go, Dear," I said, "my day was wonderful."

"What did you do?"

"I stayed here in the house. I straightened out some things, putting them back in their correct places. Other things I must have disturbed slightly."

"Ah, good. That sounds good. Did you think of me? I thought of you once, while I was handing out tests in class."

This kind of closing to the day started me thinking, about the repetition of things.

She turned up at the most unfortunate times, random times. Once about thirty years before, I was out dancing with a young man named Rudy. He was tall, fair, so thin there seemed little place for his gender; he wore a navy blue pinstripe suit. I was in black, and he held me around the waist with his long arms, smiling mysteriously. Now and again Rudy would kiss me, and I would kiss back with force, but I wanted more to shout: the jig was up, to hell with all of that! The blind husband was at home listening to the victrola, not the least bit worried over my disappearance.

But I didn't shout. I drank. And I enjoyed being the belle of his ball, the femme fatale. He took my hands in his and I spun under and around and fainted dead away from drunkenness.

I came to in Rudy's arms; he was carrying me to a table against the wall. The room was applauding.

"Oh, don't worry," said Rudy. "They took it for a dance move. You can't misstep, can you? I've never seen anything like it! It's as if you had more than two feet. That's it! You have three feet! Perhaps even four!"

I told him he was too kind, and I didn't stop him when I felt his roughened cheeks beneath my chin, at my neck. As the spinning slowed, though, I pushed his face away, and watched the crowd in the dance hall. I watched as one woman was lifted high by supporting hands at her pelvis, high above the crowd, spun in ballet style, around the head of a handsome, tall man. He carried her in that position straight through the crowd, not twenty feet from me, and out the door.

It was my twin.

"What is she doing here?" I whispered.

"What do you mean?" said Rudy.

"What's she doing here?"

"Calm," he said. He started in on my neck again. "Never mind. Never mind, little puppet."

She had blonde hair like mine, probably gone silver. But she was right-handed while I am the opposite. Is it correct to assume than that the now slack right side of my face, where the tic has set in, is matched by an equal and opposite tic in the left side of her face? Is my simultaneous desire for and antipathy toward her matched by an opposite set of sentiments? Isn't it because of her that I am reduced to all of this?

I asked all these questions at one time or another.

He cut his mutton daintily. We were silent a while. It was just past sunset. In the library, the phonograph sawed away at a chamber music record of his.

"I think," he said, "that I'd like to put some flowers out in front. In a little box perhaps."

"I think that's lovely," I said. "But what's your interest in flowers?"

"What do you mean by that?" he said, dabbing at the corner of his mouth with a napkin. "I can enjoy the idea of flowers, can't I? There isn't, it's true, much of an actual flower for me, but the idea remains, anyway. I'd like to be reminded of that idea."

I reached for my wine. "But I'll have to water them, or else watch them die."

"Luck of the draw," he said. "Materiality is gotten at a high price."

I served him some more.

"Although I suppose," he said. "I suppose you could fib about the flowers. You could say that you had the flower box built and then forget all about it, as I probably will, or you could describe to me, in literary detail our fictional pansies and petunias without lifting a finger. The effect would be the same for me."

"My god," I said. "Flowers live and die for you in seconds. Would you mind doing the dishes for me that way?"

"Dear," he said, "you underestimate your imaginative powers."

[. . .]

I pushed my little shopping cart across the electronic mat that opened the electronic door. There was a synthetic ripping sound and a door opened, while another slid shut behind me. I rolled my cart forward.

Entering, through the adjacent glass doors, in a pink raincoat and scarf, it was her. I tried to go back through the "out" door, but it wouldn't give, and by the time

I had abandoned my cart and run to the entrance, she had snuck inside and ducked around the check-cashing center.

A blue car pulled up in front of my shopping cart. A heavy man, in an old maroon sweater with patches on the elbows, got out, and started putting my bags in the trunk.

"Excuse me," I said, out of breath.

"You phone for a cab?"

"Well, no, I was about to, though. How did you know? And how did you know those were my bags, before I even got here?"

He looked at me.

"How did you know?"

He put the last bag in the trunk, and walked around to the driver's seat.

"You want a cab?" he said, over the roof. "I'm a cab."

"Do you have a message for me?" I shouted at last. "Do you have a message for me from my twin?"

"Message nothing," said the maroon sweater. "Your husband called I guess. Some guy. Said to get you and your groceries. Said to say he would probably be late. I thought if you didn't come out I'd take the goddamn groceries myself."

With that, he jumped in, and gunned the engine. With that, I sat in that back, feeling a bit weaker.

At six, I lit the candles for dinner. I didn't worry that he was late, but merely hoped that he was lost in a flattering place. Not out drinking with the other blind professors, or chatting with some remedial student, but perhaps standing on a corner listening to a classical trio.

When I opened the door at sunset to turn on the porch light, he was lying on his side on the front step. For I don't know how long.

I took him right to bed. He didn't look so well. I took his sunglasses off and wiped his forehead. The eyes were reddish and they rolled about independently.

"What shall I do?"

"I don't care," he said. "I'm going to sleep." I lifted him to his feet, and half-dragged him up the stairs to the bedroom. "Oh, by the way," he said, partway up, "did you get the cab?"

"Quiet," I said.

I slipped into my nightgown and got into bed. In a minute he was sleeping soundly, and even as I held tight as I could, it was like lying against nothing at all. There wasn't much to separate that calm from his death.

"It was a surprise, wasn't it?" he slurred. "I did it with electronics. With mirrors."

But I am not alone now, either. I am not alone.

EIGHTH GRADE JOURNAL

ISAAC FITZGERALD has been a firefighter, worked on a boat, and been given a sword by a king, thereby accomplishing three of his five childhood goals. He has written for the *Bold Italic*, *McSweeney's*, *Mother Jones*, and the *San Francisco Chronicle*. He is the books editor for BuzzFeed.com.

[Note from Isaac's mom, Susan: "Sagging neckline on T-shirt denotes his chewing on collars is still an oral pastime. (Not yet smoking???)]

This is something I wrote for a class, which meant that in eighth grade I was handing it in to a teacher after every entry. And her name was Mrs. Jenkins, and she would then write comments. Don't forget—that's me in the photo. I'm an adorable, happy little kid.

Here's how Mrs. Jenkins started the journal: "Keeping a daily journal is very helpful in learning to become a better writer. Remember that you write best when you are interested in, and know something about, the topic you choose to write about. Think about the events and interests in your life. I am looking forward to writing and sharing with you this semester."

Clearly she had no idea what she was getting herself into. My journal quickly filled with drawings of hangmen and pentagrams on fire, poetry about drive-by shootings, and rap lyrics by the Beastie Boys.

No matter how bad it got, Mrs. Jenkins heroically tried to keep a positive outlook on my "art" by praising my vocabulary, poetic form, and attention to detail.

—I.F.

My Eigth Grade Journal

I sit here in the dark,

Not knowing were to turn,

It seems everything is wrong,

And anything I do burns,

good word!
The darkness starts to engulf me,

And   So, do you have a feeling
      I   about sending out some of
      am   your poetry, Isaac?
        at

peace.

Mrs. Jenllin's
"Engulf! Great
Word!"

Drive By

Feel the cold rain on my face,
My blood starts to pace,
Open the door and step in the car,
An AK-47 is what I saw,
I reach for it as I sit,
I was scared but now I don't give a shit,
The store is what we drive by,
The bullets start to fly,
People cry,
While they die,
I sigh,
And try not to cry.

⭐ This poem is interesting.
You have tackled a tough topic.
Question: If the speaker
of the poem is the
drive by shooter —
do the last 2 lines work?
Comment: A worthy subject.
Keep writing.

STEPHEN ELLIOTT

IT'S DUMB

STEPHEN ELLIOTT's books include *Happy Baby*, *My Girlfriend Comes to the City and Beats Me Up*, and *The Adderall Diaries*. Elliott is the director of the movie *About Cherry* and an adaptation of his novel *Happy Baby*. His writing has been featured in *Esquire*, the *New York Times*, the *Believer*, *GQ*, *The Best American Nonrequired Reading 2005* and *2007*, *The Best American Erotica*, and *Best Sex Writing 2006*. He is also the founding editor of the popular online literary magazine the *Rumpus*.

I started writing poetry when I was about ten or eleven. When I was twelve, I started going over to my friend Dave Dorocke's house, and I would read my poetry to his mom. We would smoke pot together. All my other friends would be in Dave's room listening to thrash metal, while I was in the living room with his mom, smoking pot and reading poetry. At the time, she wore tight jeans and she had dyed-red hair and, to me, she was a sexual being. She seemed to really like my poetry.

When I was thirteen, I ran away from home and I was sleeping on the streets for a while. I left my poems with Mrs. Dorocke, and then she gave them back to me. I left Chicago and hitchhiked to California when I was fourteen, and in East L.A. a trucker stole my bag with all my poems in it.

But it turned out that Mrs. Dorocke had made copies of all my poetry. And a few years ago, she sent me all my poems back. It was about that time when I realized she was either a very nice person or she was delusional. I'm going to say she was very nice. She put a cover on it—an image of a skeleton hand-cutting roses. A lot of the poems are very dark.

There is no doubt in my mind that going to Mrs. Dorocke's house and reading my poems, having her tell me how good they were, and getting that female attention is the reason I became a writer.

—S.E.

```
                  IT'S   DUMB


      It's a trip, but that's not it.

   Where am I at, I'm so high.

   I'm above the sky!

   What I'm trying to say is...

   You won't listen...Anarchy's revolution has risen.

   The time will come—then you won't scoff.

   I see your all fools letting the King...

   Steal all your jewels.

   If you die young...you stay young.

   If you die old...you mold.

   Do you think it matters if you find me in 2000 years.

   If you read my poems or discover my tears?


            COPYWRITE 1986-
```

WENDY MacNAUGHTON

ART SCHOOL EMO

WENDY MacNAUGHTON is an illustrator. Her drawings and illustrated journalism can be seen in places like the *New York Times*, the *Wall Street Journal*, and *Print* magazine. She has illustrated several books, including *Lost Cat: A True Story of Love, Desperation, and GPS Technology*; *The Essential Scratch and Sniff Guide to Becoming a Wine Expert*; *Meanwhile in San Francisco: The City in Its Own Words*; and *Pen & Ink: Tattoos and the Stories Behind Them*. Her work has been anthologized in both *The Best American Infographics* and *The Best American Nonrequired Reading 2013*. She lives in San Francisco with her partner, the writer Caroline Paul.

This is a self-portrait: me hitting on me. From learning to do double exposure in photography.

///

Art school teaches you many things about making art. How light hits a sphere and casts a shadow. How to mix every color you need out of five tubes of paint. How to capture the contours of fabric on the page without looking at your paper. And how to shoot, edit, and screen video art so terrible that should anyone uncover it later in your lifetime, it could be used as blackmail.

But more than making art, art school teaches you how to be an art student. For example:

1. How to look discontented without looking like you're trying too hard.
2. How to have disdain for everything. Except David Byrne. Then especially David Byrne. Then except David Byrne.

3. Anything can be art. (Especially when you only have five minutes before class and something's due.)

4. No matter how many times you try to convince them otherwise, neither your angst nor your dream interpretations are of interest to your instructors. But you keep trying. With lots of self-portraits.

5. That sooner or later you have to grow up, scrap the emo junk, learn your art history, realize it's a business, and start making really bad conceptual art.

The piece here was made when I was firmly rooted in number 4, just prior to learning number 5.

I call this *Self-Portrait: Art School, Semester 1.*

—W.M.

DAMIAN ROGERS

PERSEPHONE

DAMIAN ROGERS was born and raised in suburban Detroit and is now based in Toronto, where she occasionally writes lyrics for Canadian troubadours. Her first book of poetry, *Paper Radio*, was nominated for the Pat Lowther Memorial Award. She is the creative director of Poetry in Voice/Les Voix de la Poésie, a recitation contest for high school students in Canada, and the poetry editor at House of Anansi Press. She has been preparing since the 1980s for a cameo in a Jim Jarmusch film. He still hasn't called.

//

I asked my friend Brett if he had a copy of one of my terrible high school poems (he's a natural archivist, so there was a chance), and he came back with this thing that I'd completely forgotten existed. Oh, where to start? I was so proud of this poem that I rubber-cemented it onto purple—*purple*—card stock, which I carefully decorated with paint splotches and torn paper. Note also the jaunty placement of the poem, which further reflects my artsy instincts.

The poem itself is a classic undergraduate study of the moody, vain, self-involved drama queen (a self-portrait, naturally), all erotic innuendo and vague feminist subtext. I was obsessed with the Persephone myth, and as far as I knew, I was the only person who had the bright idea to mine this material in the first person. An innocent young girl married to Death! So sexy!

The first thing I notice about the poem is the fact that I just scissored the thing right up to its margins, revealing how little feel I had for how white space operates in a poem. (Perhaps, though, this was an echo of the claustrophobia Persephone endured in the dark and crowded Underworld? Yeah.) Also, I'm not sure the line breaks could be made any less effective than they are here. My favorite worst line is the portentous "It is time" hanging there all by itself. I bet I loved that. And I doubt I could craft a flatter line than "where my husband is."

The phrase "whispering the name of my lover" makes me shudder now, as I remember a friend from university bitingly noting, "Damian never seems to have boyfriends, just 'lovahs.'" I can't even believe I'm admitting to that in print. The shame is so intense. Additionally, the references to a "cave of shadows" and "mouth of a flower" places this work within the fine tradition of Magic Vagina poems.

I do have affection for this earlier self; I must be gentle with her. She was so unsure and awkward and so hopeful to fit in with those who don't fit in. And the presentation's craft-project, ersatz-zine aesthetic is pretty cute.

Getting back to vanity, I'm trying so hard to look like I'm living in a subtitled movie in this photo. It was taken on the fire escape of the hippie cooperative house where I lived in Ann Arbor, Michigan, in the fall of 1991. I was really into rocking "the French inhale" during this period. Oh, my Gauloises, there is no pretention like that of the nineteen-year-old would-be poet. As you can clearly see behind my head, the last leaves were holding on by their "fingernails." And you know . . . slipping.

—D.R.

Persephone

The trees are revealing their slick black bones;
the leaves are hanging on by their fingernails
and slipping.
It is time
to be buried again under my mother's rich soil
to crawl down into the cave of shadows
where my husband is.
I don't tell her but I miss the chill of his touch;
his hands are so impossibly smooth and cool
on my skin.   I sometimes dreamed
about the damp smell of his world
even as I burned under the August light,
lying in a sea of sharp grass.
I fell into his world through the mouth of a flower
that opened up like a trap door
swallowing me, changing me.
The air is changing now, blowing faster
and whispering the name of my lover
into my tingling ear.

AMONG THE BARBARIANS

ROBERT ANASI

ROBERT ANASI is the author of *The Gloves: A Boxing Chronicle* and *The Last Bohemia: Scenes from the Life of Williamsburg, Brooklyn*. His third book of nonfiction, *Golden Man: The Remarkable Quest of Gene Savoy*, is suffering in a strange publishing purgatory, where it awaits redemption. Anasi's journalism, criticism, and reviews have appeared in many publications, including the *New York Times*, the *Times Literary Supplement*, *Virginia Quarterly Review*, the *New York Observer*, the *Los Angeles Times*, *Salon*, and *Publishers Weekly*. He has received a New York Foundation for the Arts Fellowship, as well as a Chancellor's Club Fellowship and a Schaeffer Fellowship from the University of California, Irvine. He is a founding editor of the literary journal *Entasis*. He lives in Los Angeles but misses the Brooklyn that was.

//

Frank Lloyd Wright once said, "A doctor can always bury his mistakes. An architect can only advise his client to plant vines." For the most part, writers share the enviable position of the doctor. We used to plant our corpses in file cabinets; these days, in dustless folders that remain out of sight. At least until some grave robber like Julia Scott comes along, jostles our elbows, and makes us dig.

I brought this disfigured creature into the world at age thirty-one, years after I should have known better. As with most bad art, the impulse was noble. In college, I'd gotten bored with the standard-issue American short story. It seemed to me then (and still does) that writers were reworking mid-career Chekhov over and over and over again. I didn't see the point in writing stories that had already been written, by a genius and generations of imitators. There was no space there, and I didn't want to spend my life chasing somebody else's dragon. So I started looking at short fiction from different traditions. One thing you could say about the stories of Kafka, Borges, Márquez, and Akutagawa—narrative realism they weren't.

Unfortunately, I chose D. H. Lawrence as a model for this piece. At the time, I was under his spell. As far as I'm concerned, "The Horse Dealer's Daughter" and "Odour of Chrysanthemums" are among the most brilliant short fictions of our old English language. Lawrence can be horrible, and is, for hundreds of pages at a time, but at his best he's sui generis, jaw dropping, a miracle. That said, Lawrence is also probably inimitable. One of my biggest problems here is that in my effort to follow the master, I fall into heavy-handed Victorian-ish diction. There are other problems. Many of them. If you can stop laughing for a second, you'll see them.

—R.A.

That was how it had gone all day. He opened the door and asked how she was feeling. He asked her if she wanted to come downstairs or if she wanted him to bring her something. She would shake her head, no. Then he would sit on the edge of the bed and slip his hand under the blanket to touch her flesh. In the touch she felt his concern but as something distant. He did not regard her fully. His hand lay warm and heavy on her stomach but he did not regard her fully, not any longer. In her normal routine, she avoided that knowledge but in her sickness it pressed her and she always seemed to be sick.

Back at their apartment when she returned from work, she barely had the energy to make herself a meal. In the morning mirror her face appeared hard and lined as if she'd been drunk the night before. It was ghastly to her, the lined face in the mirror. She didn't recognize herself in that face. She was young; there was no reason for her to look like that. While she lay in bed in their apartment he roamed, vigorous and dissatisfied, walking from one little room to the next. In his pacing and sounds of frustration she saw the others in him. She could not live with that anymore. His brutality was extinguishing her.

[. . .]

It hadn't always been like that. Once his vitality had drawn her. She had sensed new possibilities through him, a new life opening through him. Together they planned to do remarkable things. When they talked the words flew and joined, forming a brief and remarkable architecture in the air. It belonged to both of them; she brought something to him as he brought something to her. And she had never met such an attractive man. She loved the way his shoulders sloped, a little apelike, and the loose way his body moved when they danced made her laugh from desire. The unhappiness came to her slowly. He grew around her, filling all the available space in the little apartment. He grew and she suffocated. Over the months, she attempted to fight her reduction but her efforts were feeble. He came from such coarseness that she could not mark him. When she pointed to his atrocities he would take shelter in the bathroom and she found herself screaming at the white paint of the door. Or he fled the apartment to return a few hours later, whistling, as if nothing had happened.

"Let's go get a drink," he would say. Her illness puzzled him and he ignored it unless she complained. He expected her to be well in a day or two and seemed oblivious as one crisis faded into the next. If he would only hold her and say, "I love you. What's wrong?" He filled their apartment as she struggled for breath. He reduced her. He took her and reduced her to a corner of his life. Some little corner where he occasionally watered her, cocked an eye at her and wandered away. In the place where she was kept he found uses for her. She made a useful extension, a pseudopod in his sprawling empire. He used her hands and mind to serve him. In bed, he ignored her and this made her hate his use of her. After the first happy months he only coupled with her rarely and then like a beast. A quick act of shame and he withdrew to an enormous distance. Still, he told her she was beautiful, he admired her skin, a thick and unmarked white. Against her pale skin her hair shone with darkness, a cloud of night against her glossy skin. She felt his admiration and could not understand why he did not desire her. She wondered what she had done to drive him away.

DO IN REMEMBRANCE

JOE LOYA

JOE LOYA is an essayist, playwright, filmmaker, actor, and the author of the memoir *The Man Who Outgrew His Prison Cell: Confessions of a Bank Robber*. Besides being a commentator on radio and TV, he has published essays in the *Los Angeles Times*, the *Washington Post*, *Utne Reader*, *Newsday*,

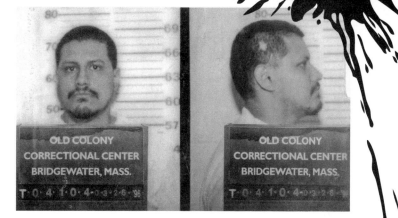

Loya's prison ID.

and *McSweeney's*. Loya published the prison zombie apocalypse novel *The Red Mile* under the pseudonym the Zombie Whisperer. Any day now he'll be done editing his short film *Animal Style*. He's currently working on a memoir about being a good father with a dark, criminal past, titled *Dada, Tell Me a Zombie Story*. He lives in the San Francisco Bay Area with his wife and daughter.

///

What you are about to read is the first short story I wrote in prison. I'd quit crime. Decided to become a writer instead. I'd come to look at the whole heist mania as bipolar grandiosity, and urgently desired to write a story that would explain how my obsession with darker themes eventually drove me mad.

I was raised by a Southern Baptist preacher. Reading the King James Bible daily was compulsory. Supplemented with nineteenth-century sermons by British preachers. My Irish stepmom fed me classic novels by Russians and French authors translated into British English. By the time I was in my teens,

I decided I wanted to be a theologian, so I got busy studying philosophy and Greek.

That's why when I started writing in prison, I could only write like those dense texts I'd cut my literary teeth on. I thought literature had to explore the greater themes, heavily reference Dostoyevsky. With an arch William Buckley-ish tone. It certainly had to have sentences interspersed with six or seven commas like my boys Henry James and James Baldwin both wrote.

Which explains why, when I found this story for *Drivel*, the following prison memory leapt to mind:

I was once offered prison wine so foul I prepared to drink it standing over my cell toilet in case I threw up. I gazed into the cup. Looked like twelve ounces of pulpy ketchup-colored vomit. I pinched my nose. Guzzled it all in two large swigs. I stamped my feet and shook my head as if two midgets were fisting my nostrils. Horrible taste. But most enjoyable drunk of my prison life.

Yeah, this story for me is like that pungent pruno. Uncomfortable like a midget fisting my nostrils. You can thank me later.

—J.L.

The photograph is slightly blemished with the distinct graininess of age, but it is still obvious to the casual viewer that in that abbreviated moment we three children were innocence personified. We three are celebrating my fifth birthday at McKenzy Park, off-balance on clumsy roller skates, wearing bright party hats, holding and hugging each other in celebration.

Marcy, K and myself all linked together: me on the left registering a goofy grimace of cooties repulsion as Marcy clutches me and plants a sloppy kiss on my cheek. On the right K is balanced by his nervous grip on the backside of her sweater, displaying a baby toothed smile with gaps, rupturing in laughter, his full eyes generously focused on the camera. I've insisted on setting this filmed memory in a frame and placing it on my desk. This is my effort to remain faithful to the old motto of the Benedictine Order: Keep Death Daily Before Your Eyes.

After school, on my front lawn, K and I would argue and wrestle like little boys often do, only to soon find Marcy beside us, first refereeing, then mimicking our stagy macho posturing. This calmed us and invariably we patched up whatever rankled us. Marcy would then set her cheap transistor radio on the porch step, turn it on and sing to us her version of some popular top-forty song. K and I twirled and danced hand in hand, in frenzied fraternal celebration like two of Snow White's lucky dwarfs enchanted to fellowship by the voice of a future princess.

Unaware of the fundamental murkiness of future, Marcy told anyone who would listen that she was going to grow up to be a ballerina. And as if in preparation for that hopeful linear advancement from desire to fulfillment, her parents enrolled her in tap dance lessons at age four. She was always eager to enrich us with a demonstration of her most recent dance lesson. It wasn't an uncommon scene to find her somewhere on the road home from school, in the center of a crowd of children, dancing on a patch of a neighbor's property, swiveling her formless hips, slowly arching her valiant miniature arms above her head like a the delicate unfolding of a Japanese paper-fan.

When K and I were six years old we joined the tiny-tot football league. Our team scrimmaged each Saturday morning and Marcy would be on the sideline, an energetic maestro in bold huzzah, orchestrating the corps of six-year old cheerleaders.

The year that we were supposed to graduate from Washington Elementary School, a stranger abducted Marcy from a local Foster Freeze parking lot on her way home from school. Three weeks later her remains were found by a sanitation employee during his usual collection rounds in a local alley. She had been sexually assaulted and butchered, swaddled in six separate bedspreads, wrapped in trash bags, then dumped in two garbage cans. Identical notes tied to each of the six bags read: "Six is the number of man."

Throughout Washington Elementary and Luther Burbank Junior

High School years, K and I were closer than brothers and often confused as such. Being next-door neighbors made our daily frolic conducive to the adventurous bonding of boyhood. Fishing at the local creek. Sleeping overnight in a tent near the quarry. The mutual loss of our playmate also cemented our unity.

I have for some time now toyed with timeframes and fragments of early conversations with K in order to find and amplify any nuance that might suggest or determine the genesis of his surrender to a renegade deprivation as a combat technique against unrestrained grief. My recollections take me back to a choking colloquy on football bleachers several years after Marcy's death. That particular sophomore afternoon hinted at an alteration in the wind.

We sat apart from our teammates, uniformed in full gear and waiting for the coaches to arrive to our practice from some emergency that had delayed them. To a stranger we would have appeared to them as two young gladiators pondering strategies for the arena—and the stranger would have been partially correct.

"Do you miss Marcy?"

There was an uncharacteristic bullying insinuation in the way he asked the question and I remember feeling uncomfortably challenged when I answered him.

"Of course I miss her."

He paused and looked at the team playbook tossed beside us. His tense edge withered.

"It's been five years since she died and something bad is happening to me. I feel like I got some malevolent virus growing in me."

His parents were professors so his elocution often resounded with maturity.

I reveled in the shift of attention, secretly reluctant not to have my grief be the focal point of conversation. I half-heartedly placated him.

"C'mon K, you don't really mean that."

"Don't do that. Don't dismiss me. This is very serious and complicated. I miss her very much, it's just that, well, lately I find myself concentrating for hours exclusively on my private pain, not even thinking about how it is her loss that brought on the pain in the first place. It's become about me only."

He was grinding his teeth as he stared through his helmet, mesmerized by a distant point in the horizon.

"Her loss hurts me so much that I sometimes wish that I didn't have the memory of her at all."

A few moments of silence passed between us and he picked up his thought again.

"Nobody could have stopped her killer's urges or his sickness, his evil, but in my mind, and I know this is gonna sound horrible, I wish it would have happened to someone else, anybody else, Shelly Longing in homeroom for example, any girl but our Marcy. And I wish this sometimes in the dark moments so that her killer could have spared me, as much as her, the misery."

He choked and reached a fist through his helmet, smearing tears across his cheeks. My throat constricted.

He mumbled, "Did you hear what I just said? Shelly Longing? She didn't ever do anything to me. It's wrong for me to think that way. Wrong, wrong wrong, and I'm simply no good anymore. I'm polluted with this virus-like grief."

The integrity of his remorse provoked a deep sympathy in me and for a Spartan moment I fought back tears.

"That's not true. You're very good K. C'mon, this is really tough on both of us because we were so close to her. You've got to quit being so hard on yourself."

He ignored me and recovered deftly.

"You don't understand the evil implications of my thinking. When I substitute Shelly for Marcy that already puts me on some continuum with the serial killer who killed Marcy. My flagrant selfishness projects the gruesome act on an innocent person and this kind of insane vision frightens me. My instinct is becoming demented."

"You've got to stop torturing yourself with that sort of thinking. Listen to me K, she was too good for this world so the gods took her to be with them. That's what I believe and that belief comforts me whenever I miss her."

"I hate that man, and god damn it, I hate this. It's like I need to insulate myself from too much suffering. I don't want to know any more victims."

He rose crying and mumbling to either God or himself, "I can't do this, I can't do this, I can't do this."

He picked up the playbook, swooned in incoherent shame, and in almost comical ambulatory leisure he meandered across the field to the locker room, thus ending his promising athletic career. My friend's imagination was mounting Elijah's same chariot, readying itself for delirious empyrean heights. And behind would remain a human shell and mocking jape, cruel evidence of the gods' attempt at high comedy.

6

TERRIBLE ANGST

What would she say to Linzee Lawley, a beautiful, popular cheerleader?

—Gillian Flynn

TROUBLE AT OSAGE LAKE HIGH

GILLIAN
FLYNN

GILLIAN FLYNN is the author of *Sharp Objects*, *Dark Places*, and the number-one *New York Times* bestseller *Gone Girl*, which has sold more than 6 million copies worldwide. She is also the screenwriter for the film adaptation of *Gone Girl*. Flynn lives with her family in Chicago, where she may or may not be hoarding every single original paperback of Sweet Valley High ever.

///

In junior high, the primary topic on my mind was figuring out How to Be a Cool Teen. I know this because in the same ancient Garfield Trapper Keeper in which I unearthed "Trouble at Osage Lake High," I found a self-improvement list titled "Changes." Some useful entries: "Hair: Buy and experiment with mousse." "Conversation: Think of interesting things to talk about. Listen to friends' conversations. Practice."

Yes, I was a painfully shy kid, and so I looked for guidance in books. Specifically, that soapy staple of the '80s: the Sweet Valley High series, which beckoned readers to follow "the continuing story of the Wakefield twins—their laughter, heartaches, and dreams." It was basically *Dynasty* in high school. Actually it was better, because it starred good and evil twins. (Is there anything more satisfying than good and evil twins? We'll answer this question shortly.) Jessica Wakefield was the wild one (on the illustrated cover, her blond hair is moussey-loose over her jean jacket) and Elizabeth was the nice twin (her blond hair clipped back in sensible barrettes). I was obsessed with Sweet Valley High—reading the books wasn't just fun, it was obligatory prep work. What I learned from them was that my high school years would revolve around cheerleading, being beautiful, betraying friends, and fighting over boys. Cool!

Naturally, they influenced my burgeoning career as a writer. (Was I a "Jessica" or an "Elizabeth"? The fact that I was in eighth grade and launching my own book series probably answers that question.) So, in answer to the earlier query: Is there anything better than good and evil twins? Ladies and gentlemen, I present to you: good, evil, and goodish-evil *triplets*! Sit back and enjoy "the continuing story of the Lawley triplets—their bickering, kissing, and . . . German lessons." With my apologies.

—G.F.

"Tru! Tru, don't walk away when I'm talking to you." Tru Lawley swirved around, a cascade of black curls swirling about her shoulders.

"Geez, Hope, sometimes you sound just like my mom."

"Your not getting out of it that easy, Tru. You were kissing my boyfriend, remember? Any particular reason?"

"Hope, your precious, darling boyfriend was kissing me, I mean he practically jumped me!"

"And, of course, you didn't discourage him." Hope Wexler's green eyes sparkled with sarcasm.

"Hope, who are you going to believe: your boyfriend of two weeks or your friend of well, birth! Talk to Matt if you want to get to the bottom of it—I don't know why he kissed me." Tru's dark brown eyes lowered, spilling tears down her pink cheeks.

"I'm sorry Tru, I guess I just wanted to hide myself as to what Matt's really like." Hope put a comforting arm around her friend. "Now you better hurry or you'll be late. I'll talk to you at lunch."

"He just wouldn't stop, Hope," Tru started for German. "Of course he didn't have any objections from me," she thought, a sly look replacing the cherubic smile she'd worn seconds ago. Tru daydreamed her way through German, very aware of the fact that Matt Davenport, football star and resident hunk, was paying much more attention to her than the lesson.

Midway through chapter seven, a piece of paper was tossed her way. WHY DID YOU KISS ME? was scrawled in big blue letters. You kissed me, lied Tru, feeling a small pang of guilt. But how much harm could one little kiss do? Matt hadn't exactly pulled away. The bell rang, and Tru tried to hurry on but Matt caught up with her in the hall.

"I kissed you? That's a good one." Tru tried to charm her way out of the potentially dangerous situation.

"Well you know Matt, the good guy image of yours WAS getting a bit boring." She stroked his hair. "Besides, it wasn't planned, just one of those impulsive things I do. I mean, your too goodlooking for your own good." He dark eyelashes fluttered at him, she leaned carefully against her locker.

Matt slowly smiled. "Tru? You know what?"

"What?" She smiled seductively.

"Tru, sometimes you make me sick." Matt Davenport walked on, probably looking for Hope.

Tru's cheeks lit up in a streak of red. She let out a stream of curses as she looked through her untidy locker.

"Hey, Lawley, I need to talk to you." Three beautiful girls turned around simultaneously. Cory Overly grinned. "Sorry, I just need to talk to one out of the set. Kit, the Drama Department is deciding on the musical for this year and they wanted your vote. Said to stop in after school."

Cory smiled tenderly at Kit. He kissed her on the nose. Then lowered to kiss her on the lips. Linzee Lawley clapped.

"What is this? A family peepshow?" Cory grinned. "Boy, dating Kit Lawley keeps me busy enough but I can't wait till I get to date Kit, Linzee, and Tru Lawley. I can just hear it now: who are you dating Cory? Oh, just the Lawley triplets." His eyes sparkled mischievously.

"Come on Romeo," said Kit. "Let's get lunch."

Though it was common to call Kit, Linzee and Tru "The Lawley Triplets," they could hardly be grouped into a nice neat category. It was like comparing a quiet spring day, a breezy afternoon, and a stormy night. Linzee Lawley was mild, sensible, cheerful and liked to keep things simple. She possessed all-American good looks: wavy chin-length gold-brown hair, light green eyes, and a slender 5'4" figure that was shown off beautifully by her cheerleading outfit. She was easy to talk to, a fact which gave her great status at Osage Lake High.

Kit was outspoken, independent, charming, and interested in every-thing. She was president of the Drama Club, was a photographer for the yearbook and star of Osage Lake High's track team. She had sparkling baby blue eyes, straight shoulder length wheat-blonde hair and a tan toned 5'6" figure that was put to advantage by the short skirts she loved to wear.

Then there was the not-so-mild Tru. Tru loved attention and was always at the top of the list of "A-Rank" girls at Osage (often just tying with, instead of beating her sisters, to her frustration.) Tru was daring, wild, and usually behind and mischief occurring at the high school. She usually managed to get everything she wanted—a fact that had a lot to do with her spectacular looks. She was 5'8" with jet black curls spilling almost to the middle of her back. Dark amber eyes were framed by long black lashes. She had a peaches and cream complexion and a dazzling smile—used to its full advantage, of course. Right now though, Tru's lips were in a becoming pout.

"Okay, Tru, spill it," Linzee Lawley's voice was light but concerned.

"Matt Davenport is such a jerk!"

"What'd he do?"

"Trust me Linzee, he's just a jerk."

"Could it perhaps have anything to do with that incredible kiss ear-lier?" Linzee's voice dripped with disapproval.

"That was as much his fault as it was mine. More!" Snapped Tru.

"Tru, come on, I saw you before you kissed him, you were looking for him. The whole thing was planned, it was obvious!"

Tru knew she was cornered. "Well come on Linzee, do you think Matt and Hope go together? I mean, she is pretty and she's one of my best friends but they just aren't right for each other."

"One, that decision should be left up to Matt and Hope. Two, I'd bet you haven't even thought about wether they're right for each other—I bet you just saw something you liked and went after it. Did you even think of the effect it could have on Hope?"

"Well nothing happened, so forget it!"

"I just don't understand how you can do this to your friend."

"Damn you, Linzee! You never even listen to my side!" Tru stormed away, colliding into Ivy Webber, a quiet sophomore. "Watch it!"

Ivy mumbled an apology, then sighed. It seemed the only time some-one like Tru Lawley talked to her was to tell her to get out of the way. Then Ivy saw Linzee sitting beside her own locker, her eyes full of tears. She was going to keep on walking, what would she say to Linzee Lawley, a beautiful, popular cheerleader? But something about the girl made Ivy change her mind.

"Uh, Linzee, are you OK?" She asked hesitantly. Linzee looked up, surprised.

"Yeah, it's just my sister, she really has a temper." Linzee smiled behind her tears, she sun coming out after the rain. Ivy was surprised to hear Linzee tell her the whole story unhesitantly.

"Well," Ivy started, "I don't think the argument was your fault at all."

"But Tru was right, I really didn't give her the benefit of the doubt."

"Well she can't stay mad long," Ivy suggested.

"Tru will either come up to me after school like nothing happened or she won't talk to me for weeks. But I'll worry later. It's one extreme or the other with her."

STEVE ALMOND

TO THE MEN AT WORK OUTSIDE MY WINDOW

STEVE ALMOND is the author of ten books of fiction and nonfiction, most recently the story collection *God Bless America*. His memoir *Candyfreak* was a *New York Times* bestseller. His short stories have appeared in the Best American and Pushcart anthologies. He lives outside Boston with his wife and their three kids, none of whom are bad poets. Yet.

'm not sure where to begin. This poem is like a very serious cancer, or perhaps several cancers at once. Or maybe it's my way of announcing that I deserve cancer. It's hard to say anything definitive amid so many bad judgments.

Witness this narrative of cultural encounter in which the effete, lonely Bad Poet typecasts the working-class palookas in a manner that is at least as bigoted—more so, actually—than the targets of his princely consideration. Upon further review, this "poem" is not only self-aggrandizing and pretentious (hell, that's just the color of my ink, folks) but demeaning and oddly homophobic. I'm just that good.

I do remember the episode that triggered this poem's composition. I was around thirty-five, living in Somerville, Massachusetts, and trying to be a writer. I was lying in my bed, depressed, again, when a fleet of workers turned up to tear apart the backyard of the house I was renting. This was all being done at the be-hest of my landlord, a monumental American who blew through his mortgage loans with a dizzying and tender devotion to personal bankruptcy. Trucks he bought and canoes and boats and race cars whose monstrous flatulent engines he revved at all hours outside my bedroom, with its dark wainscoting and low beams.

Was there anything I might have said to these guys beyond the obvious? That I was lonely and inept, that I envied them their camaraderie, their mas-culine competence. That I viewed them as stand-ins for the brothers whom I had resented and pined for throughout my childhood. It was their fault (the brothers, the workmen) that I felt weak and effeminate and unworthy of love. It was their fault we destroyed one another. It's always someone else's fault. That's the lesson history teaches the aggrieved, over and over.

"Is there nothing between us besides cocks?" That's an illicit wish posing as an indignant question. But the Bad Poet has no access to the mysteries of his in-ternal life, so he settles for bad jokes about classic rock and fake lyricism. It might even be okay to pity him, if he didn't so obnoxiously assert pity as his birthright.

—S.A.

To the Men at Work Outside My Window

See here, fellows: It is me, your skinny-stemmed little daisy faggot boy
Yoo-hoo! Yes, me—the fellow you keep glaring at.
I have a few things to say, if I might.
Might I? Right, then: first off, let me accede to the discrepancies
between us. I did not just recently fall from the turnip truck,
or what have you. I can see, from the cut of the collective jib
out your way, the paintsplat and jeanrip, those ungodly scabs,
that we are not destined for tea,
okay? Understood. Capiched. Comprendo'ed.

There are divisions here deeper than language, or drill bits

Yes yes. We would tire of one another in a matter of minutes

You would bang and I would frill

bang bang

frill frill

And never the twain shall meet

But say: since you have knocked me awake and into this dew-clingy day

I find myself gilding a few questions

As in: all that banging and haranguing

is it all entirely necessary to the repairs you have been summoned here
        to enact

And: why are you all named Richie?

Is there some sort of law—the law of Richies?

And: why all the niggers and spics and chinks and so forth

Some of my best friends, you understand,

they are niggers and spics and chinks

and they know how to use sanders, some of them

And the cadences of your speech (which are rhythm type things)

How do you do that, each and every day,

murdering all those syllables?

Are you aware that the letter "r" is still in wide use?

And classic rock?

How many times the rising sun and the hotel in California and who,
        precisely, is wrapped up in that goddamned douche?

Don't you ever feel just a bit numb?

Don't you ever get tired of your tools?

Don't you ever, in some secret sun, sit in wonder of the leaves?

or the women you undress around your offbrand cigarettes

Is it all just sawdust and Sheetrock?

Is there nothing between us besides cocks?

And what lies beneath all that sun-puckered skin?

Can your blood, ever, be had by something less than knuckles?

COLD SHOWERS AND IMAGINARY FRIENDS

JOSHUA MOHR

JOSHUA MOHR is the author of four novels, including *Damascus*, which the *New York Times* called "Beat-poet cool." He's also written *Some Things That Meant the World to Me*, one of *O, The Oprah Magazine*'s Top 10 reads of 2009 and a *San Francisco Chronicle* bestseller, as well as *Termite Parade*, an Editors' Choice on the *New York Times* bestseller list. He lives in San Francisco and teaches in the MFA program at University of San Francisco. His latest novel is *Fight Song*.

///

ere's the thing: I want to lie to you. I want so badly to tell you I wrote this when I was in junior high. That way, you'd nod and smirk and shake your head at the bad prose we construct in adolescence. You'd give me the benefit of the doubt, knowing we've all scribbled a few embarrassing lines way back when we wore braces.

Problem is that I wrote this when I was twenty. Twenty! Living in the Lower Haight. Dreadlocked. Drinking forty ouncers and reading the Beats and writing the worst poetry ever. I can't tell you any more details from that era because I don't remember. If pushed on it, I could say this—be careful who you idolize, or maybe you'll end up living in some Bukowski-inspired squalor, only to find out it's not charming or hilarious to be a broke alcoholic. That's a hole it takes years to dig yourself out of, and maybe I'm still digging.

Anyway, I soon realized that my gifts on the page were best served in the novel form and I retired my "poetry pen." But for all of you who've never met a car crash you won't gawk at, please meet my wreck.

—J.M.

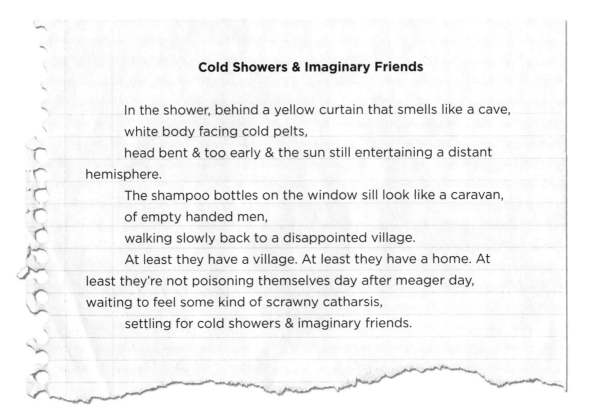

Cold Showers & Imaginary Friends

In the shower, behind a yellow curtain that smells like a cave,
white body facing cold pelts,
head bent & too early & the sun still entertaining a distant
hemisphere.
The shampoo bottles on the window sill look like a caravan,
of empty handed men,
walking slowly back to a disappointed village.
At least they have a village. At least they have a home. At
least they're not poisoning themselves day after meager day,
waiting to feel some kind of scrawny catharsis,
settling for cold showers & imaginary friends.

TISSUES

MATTHEW ZAPRUDER

MATTHEW ZAPRUDER is the author of four collections of poetry, most recently *Come On All You Ghosts* (a *New York Times* Notable Book of the Year) and *Sun Bear.* A professor in the St. Mary's College of California MFA program and English department, he is also an editor at Wave Books. He lives in Oakland, California.

wrote this poem in the spring of 1989, when I was a senior at Amherst College. I was in the first poetry writing class I had ever taken, a workshop with the Polish poet Piotr Sommer, whose reasonable reaction to our privileged and uninformed versification could be described as mildly despairing ennui.

The accompanying photo is my senior picture. It seems I am inexplicably wearing a kind of motley collision of various late-'80s collegiate uniforms: rolled-up and pegged army pants, cheap Chinese slippers I bought on Canal Street in Manhattan, a ratty cardigan, and unfortunately, a blue bandanna, Axl Rose–style. I loved (and still love) Guns N' Roses. At the time I did not realize how ill-advised it was to translate this musical admiration into a sartorial choice. I also didn't realize that the most famous writer alum of Amherst, David Foster Wallace, had also worn a similar do-rag.

The first thing to notice is that "tissues" liberates itself immediately and pointlessly from the prison of capitalization. The poem begins by addressing an unspecified "you." It's pretty clear that the "speaker" in the poem (me) is displeased with the behavior of this presumably female person.

After extensive forensic research, I have determined that in the fifth stanza I crossed out the word "nose" and changed it to the far more powerful "snot." The emotional state of the speaker—attractive woundedness? repressed rage?— is glaringly enacted by the dramatic repetition of "over / and over / and over / again."

The poem concludes with a line break that seems (like most of the other breaks in the poem) to portend some sort of leap into the unknown, or at least something surprising, when actually the next word is exactly the one that you would most expect. This seems to be the formal enactment of the emotional position of the poem: the speaker thinks he is being dramatically hurt and attractive, when actually he is just being silly and obvious, even unintentionally funny.

It's kind of upsetting for me to read this poem and realize that on the other end of it there was an actual young woman, with feelings and insecurities, something I am quite sure never occurred to me. I don't know if I ever actually gave this to anyone, and I can't remember who the lucky lady was to whom this was addressed. Whoever she was, I'd just like to apologize to her for treating her like an object in my private drama. I was just trying to work something out.

—M.Z.

"tissues"

you use
your friends
like tissues.

people are
very definitely
fragile

you tear holes
in them

by
bringing them
very close
to your beautiful
face

and then
blowing
your
~~the~~ snot
all over them

you do this
over
and over
and over
again

you must
have
a
very
bad

cold.

ANITA AMIRREZVANI

FUGITIVE FANCY

ANITA AMIRREZVANI was born in Tehran, Iran, and raised in San Francisco. Her first novel, *The Blood of Flowers*, has appeared in twenty-five languages and was long-listed for the 2008 Orange Prize for Fiction. Her second novel, *Equal of the Sun*, was published in 2012. *Tremors: New Fiction by Iranian American Writers*, an anthology she coedited with Persis Karim, was released in 2013 by the University of Arkansas Press. Amirrezvani teaches at the California College of the Arts.

No matter what you do, don't try to resuscitate your nineteen-year-old self. Never dig into that box of college papers that you've kept for more than thirty years, only to be reminded that not only did you write a piece of fiction with the dreadful title of "Fugitive Fancy," but that it's a rewrite of a draft that was even worse. Don't keep digging, because you might discover that your Vassar College fiction-writing professor, whose name you will have forgotten, has written two pages of wise advice about your first draft, which you were far too inexperienced to understand; that he has made a list of eighteen "vague" adjectives in your work to demonstrate to you what good writing is; that his comments are encouraging, demanding, and precise, as if you were a real writer; that he is big-hearted enough to praise your second draft for being "rich in suggestiveness" but begs you to "shorten this, and get it all direct, credible, consistent in diction and tone"; that he longs for you to "show it, don't tell it"; and finally, that he has spent far more time on your work than your fledgling effort deserves. Never go on to become a professor yourself—of writing no less—and try to match his generosity, humanity, and tough love in your comments to your own students, because you'll be doomed to fail.

Thank you, Professor X. You don't know me (and I hope you don't remember me), but I love you.

—A.A.

Fugitive Fancy

Andrei sat sipping his coffee in an outdoor café in the Latin Quarter. The sputtering sound of the expresso machine reached him through the din of conversation and the rich aroma of coffee filled his nostrils. Waves of light brown hair softened the sharp angles of his face and his full, blood-red lips stood out like a wound in skin ivory white and translucent. His square chin and gaunt cheeks made him ressemble a bust of Roman antiquity. A silk scarf was knotted loosely about his neck and fluttered gently as he breathed. His eyes were drawn by the play of passersby who paraded up and down the narrow street, by the flicker of light and shadow in the folds of garments and in the creases of expression.

All heads in the café were angled to observe the stream of color and variety that passed before them. Rue de la Huchette was well known for its lighted taverns and lively restaurants, but its main attraction was the people who came to see each other and to be part of the scene and the gaiety.

A woman walked through the crowd's gaze, her heels tapping and echoing on the cobblestones, her hair tossing and swaying in rhythm with her skirt. Andrei, staring into his coffee, saw in its light cream the image of the woman, her gestures, her lightness, and all that could have been and would never be. Gone! Forever lost to him! "I could have loved her," thought Andrei, his eyes shining bright and clear with sudden sorrow. He saw himself leap from his seat, rush out of the café and push past the swollen crowds. In the corner of his eye he perceived the swaying motion of her skirt as she turned a corner. He slowed his stride until he came abreast of the woman and breathless, looked her full in the face. When she felt his presence she stared back into his eyes. They were dark and soulful, slightly rounded and set deeply into his face, so dark that the pupil and the iris seemed one. Her reflection was mirrored there, clear and bright as on the surface of shiny marble. And so she sunk into their depths, enthralled by the smooth and unwavering image of herself.

The sharp notes of a pinball machine stirred him from his revery. His legs were tense and trembling, and unfulfilled desire settled in him like dark heavy clouds. He felt it thick and bitter in his throat and chest. In his hand a pack of cigarettes was crushed and mutilated, and his palm was dark with the crescent-shaped imprint of his nails. Slowly he released it and let it drop from his limp hand. He picked up his spoon and stirred his coffee until the cream became white swirls in the dark liquid, and the image of the woman faded and flew from his fancy.

Andrei paid his bill and took leave of the café. Tree-lined boulevards stretched before him, their lighted taverns an invitation to folly. He turned his back on the city and started up the winding street, the presence of the church of St. Severin closing around him amid the gaiety and laughter that emanated from the jazz clubs and the milling crowds. Turning away from the street that led to the church's door, he passed brightly-lit Greek taverns displaying red raw meat on skewers and whole pigs lying agape, their mouths stuffed with apples.

Andrei pushed himself into the niche of a building and ran his fingers over the cold stone. Its alternating surfaces of smooth and rough recalled the bittersweet memories of youth. When he was a child, his grandmother had taken him to market every Sunday morning. He remembered carrying her wicker basket with pride while she chose the best fruits and vegetables. But sometimes he felt small and weak in the bustling crowds and he would cry and hide his face in her skirt, full of a fear he could not understand.

Andrei remained huddled in the coolness of the old stone, revering its firmness behind his back; then thrust himself into the street that led to his room. All that was life, all that was dear to him, Andrei wanted to gather now, to ascend and fly over rocky shores, the salt spray on his lips, over peaks, the snow on his lids, through forests, the smell of pine like a vacuum around him. In the darkness he perceived the figure of a young woman seated on the steps of a theatre. He slid onto the step below hers, looked up and opened his mouth to speak. The moon beamed on his face and flooded his eyes with light.

"Hello," he said. "Can I speak to you freely as one person to another?"

The girl shuddered and jerked herself to her feet, tripping over the uneven steps in an effort to get away.

"I don't want to bother you," he said softly to the fading figure. "There was something in your face that could have been dear to me. I only wanted to talk to you without any pretence or false promises."

Dark spots formed a curious pattern of circles near Andrei's worn boots. The tears hung on his lashes, waiting to be released, then washed over the lines near the corners of his mouth. He had laughed often to himself, until his sensitivity had become a hollow pit inside of him. Images of the past and future converged in a dream-life more pleasant than that elicited by human contact. No more moment's fancy would again make him vulnerable nor lead him away from his memories and dreams. He picked himself up and trudged away.

DAVID EWING DUNCAN

MY THESIS AND ME

DAVID EWING DUNCAN is an award-winning, bestselling author of eight books published in twenty-one languages. He is a correspondent for the *Atlantic* and chief correspondent for NPR's "BioTech Nation." Duncan writes for the *New York Times*, *Fortune*, *Wired*, *National Geographic*, *Discover*, and many other publications. He is a former commentator for NPR and a special correspondent and producer for ABC's *Nightline*. His latest book is *When I'm 164: The New Science of Radical Life Extension, and What Happens If It Succeeds*. He is the founding director of the Center of Life Science Policy at UC Berkeley. Duncan lives in San Francisco. His website is DavidEwingDuncan.com.

///

I'm not a procrastinator by nature, but I avoided writing my senior thesis on Ernest Hemingway until eight days before it was due. In the middle of winter break, I came back to Vassar College, looking for some peace and quiet: just me and my Olivetti typewriter, flanked by three fresh jars of Wite-Out and a stack of blank paper. It was December 31, 1979.

I had barely typed in my title before someone knocked on my door. Two neighbors and fellow thesis miscreants were headed outside in a gathering snowstorm, holding bottles of champagne and insisting that we celebrate the arrival of the 1980s.

"But . . . ," I said, eying my Olivetti.

"No buts," they said.

I'm not sure what happened next—something about mixing tequila and champagne and streaking naked in the snow. The bash drew thirty people, and eventually the Poughkeepsie police—apparently our music was so loud they could hear us more than a mile away.

What I do remember is that the next day, after the pain of a Godzilla-sized headache subsided, I wrote the epic poem "My Thesis and Me," which regrettably has survived.

—D.E.D.

This poem is dedicated to all those unfortunate souls still grinding
out those theses and also to those free individuals who have turned their
theses in and are trying to forget. The poem was written on January 14, TA 20, at
midnight.
~~Here-we-are.~~

Here we are.

My thesis and me.

My gangly desklamp and me and my theis

and me are we.

Dorms are dark at dusk as granite chapel chimes

time

for me and we.

Why die,

said I?

But we, my thesis and me, just cry.

Or sigh,

As the ivy lapped chapel chimes time for me and

of course

for we.

Grand. Why die, said I,

With a breath of death and a sigh.

Mindfuse. Fusemind.

Said me to we as we

sit voraciously on I and that breath of death and a sigh.

Black midnight trounces some onces of

of the breath of death and a sigh and I,

EVERYTHING

MAC McCLELLAND has written no poems as an adult, but as a magazine writer has won awards from the Society of Professional Journalists, the Hillman Foundation, the Online News Association, and the Society of Environmental Journalists, plus she's been nominated for two National Magazine Awards and her work has been collected in *The Best American Magazine Writing*, *The Best American Nonrequired Reading*, and *The Best Business Writing* anthologies. Her first book was a finalist for the 2011 Dayton Literary Peace Prize. Her next book is about love and post-traumatic stress disorder. Her website is Mac-McClelland.com.

MAC McCLELLAND

As my memories of how painfully shitty my high school poetry was are pretty intact, I actually refused to look at the journals I handed over to Julia Scott for *Drivel*; I only skimmed this entry, with my hands covering my groaning face, because she forced me to, and only enough to see that in it I projected all the insecurities that television had projected onto me, directly onto my then boyfriend. I wish the brilliantly titled "Everything," written when

I was fifteen, could have been, as it first appears to be, a screed against Chad (who in fact, if you called him even now would tell you, thought I was the very picture of teenage perfection) for not being able to handle me and/or accept me in all my rough, natural awesomeness. Alas, ew, it's a thank-you note for his deigning to date me. As a lot of people never outgrow that mind-set, I guess this "poem" could make me grateful that I got over that, but mostly, it makes me want to die, and never think or talk about it again, so if we ever meet on the street, please do not bring it up.

—M.M.

Everything

i know i can never be all that you want
im too bitchy, too harsh for you
i know i can never fulfull all that you need
there's things lacking, you can't deny this is true

my tongue's as quick as my temper
i say things that hurt you
you can't lie, you know you wish i'd shut up
i yell, have bad mood swings
make problems that aren't there
there's not a conversation i can't seem to fuck up

i know im too bony
a waif, as you call me
loads of bodily imperfections were tossed in
i know what you like
you can't hide you're disappointed
that i'll never have those breasts to get lost in

you wish my eyes were crystal blue
my teeth a little straighter
my attitude not quite so strong
you want my hair a little longer
& my voice a little sweet
im amazed you could stand it so long

but you seem to remain faithful

you manage to keep smiling
you sit through & endure the bad days
& im eternally grateful
that though you notice the imperfections
you see past them & love me anyways

7.95

HIPPIES

JACK BOULWARE

JACK BOULWARE is a journalist and the author/coauthor of three nonfiction books, including the Bay Area punk history *Gimme Something Better*. He is cofounder of San Francisco's annual Litquake literary festival, and its affiliated Lit Crawls in several cities, including Manhattan, Brooklyn, Seattle, Los Angeles, Iowa City, London, and Austin. As a freelance journalist he has covered stories throughout the United States and more than twenty countries. In the 1990s, he was founding editor of the satirical investigative *Nose* magazine. He lives in San Francisco and empties the trash at the Litquake office.

//

Growing up on a cattle ranch in Montana, I was always fascinated by words and books. We didn't have a TV until I was seven, so I read anything I could find, especially *National Geographic* (sharks, topless native women), and *Life* magazine (Vietnam, hippie scourge). My opinions were shaped by Walter Cronkite and various adult Montanans who most certainly had never seen either a hippie or a Black Panther.

In fourth grade, around 1970 or 1971, I synthesized all of my vast knowledge of hippies (none), wrote up this urgent little thesis, and read it aloud in front of the class. Every so often, I would find it in a box and read it again and think, Jesus, this is terrible on so many levels. The mangled spelling, the wildly inaccurate facts, the alarmist tone. I should have ended up a TV pundit.

The photo was taken on our cattle ranch in 1971. I am presenting the first fish I ever caught, a rainbow trout that I named Sam. I have since learned to use a napkin.

—J.B.

Hippies are people (usually collage students) who are against the war in Vietnam. They show it by coming in groups to Washington D.C. and starting riots. Some of them do it because they are under the influence of drugs. Common drugs are called marijuana, LSD and others. They are called heroine. Some hippies who are drug addicts will do anything to get more.

Some hippies are vandals. They ruin valuable property. The Black Panthers are Negro rioters, vandals, murders, and thiefs. They cause trouble for police and National Guard. Many police have been killed by Black Panthers.

Hippies call police

ACKNOWLEDGMENTS

It's one thing to be asked to cough up your mulligans for a humor book. It's another to do it for free. We offer our deepest respect and gratitude to all the authors who contributed deeply personal and meaningful pieces from their past to this collection, wrote thoughtful introductions, and took the time to hunt down a photo to match—taking significant pains to do so. We salute you.

For fifteen years, Litquake has brought the most exciting writers to the Bay Area and fostered the local literary community. In addition to their indefatigable work in running a premier annual literary festival and events in several cities, many staff members helped with initial author outreach for this book. Special thanks to Litquake cofounders Jack Boulware and Jane Ganahl, associate director Elise Proulx, and festival coordinators Jakki Young and Jen Siraganian.

To the Writers' Grotto community, the nuclear core at the center of all the sold-out *Regreturature* shows, not to mention much of this collection: may we continue to make beautiful fission together.

We extend our warmest appreciation to our indispensable agent, Danielle Svetcov at Levine Greenberg, and to the diligent and talented editorial and design team at Perigee Books, who used their strong creative vision to make this collection such a fun read.

Lastly, we want to give a special shout-out to all the moms who supplied vintage photos of their beloved offspring: Gillian Flynn's mom, Judith; Simon and Nathaniel Rich's mom, Gail; Isaac Fitzgerald's mom, Susan; and Julia Scott's mom, Laura.

—Julia Scott and the team at Litquake

PHOTO CREDITS

All author photos are provided courtesy of the authors unless otherwise noted.

pages x and 193: © Chris Hardy

page 75: Courtesy of Brian Kammer

ABOUT THE EDITOR

JULIA SCOTT is an award-winning radio producer, journalist, and essayist who has reported from across the United States and Canada. She has profiled giant pumpkin-growing fanatics, spent a month bathing in bacteria, and reported from the inside of an iron lung. Her work has been collected in *The Best American Science Writing*.

Scott's stories have appeared in the *New York Times*, the *New York Times Magazine*, *Modern Farmer*, *Nautilus*, *Salon*, and on PRI's Marketplace and NPR. Her BBC World Service radio documentary, "Bon Voyage," won the Excellence in Journalism Award from the NLGJA and was nominated for a Sony Radio Academy Award.

Scott hails from Montreal, Canada, and graduated from Smith College. She lives in San Francisco and is a proud member of the San Francisco Writers' Grotto. Visit her website at JuliaScott.net.

LIT●UAKE

Founded by San Francisco writers in 1999, **Litquake** has grown to become the largest independent literary festival on the West Coast. Litquake seeks to foster interest in literature for people of all ages, perpetuate a sense of literary community, and provide a vibrant forum for writing from the Bay Area and beyond, as a complement to the city's music, film, and cultural festivals. Litquake is a project of the Litquake Foundation, which also produces annual literary pub crawls, aka Lit Crawls, in San Francisco, Manhattan; Brooklyn, Austin, Iowa City, Los Angeles, Seattle, and London.

Proceeds from the sale of *Drivel* benefit the Litquake Foundation, a 501(c)3 nonprofit registered in the state of California. Visit litquake.org for more information.

The GROTTO

The San Francisco Writers' Grotto began in 1994, when Po Bronson, Ethan Watters, and Ethan Canin rented a six-room flat in a rundown Victorian on upper Market Street, to use exclusively as a workspace. From its beginnings, it has been a place where artists welcome the discipline of structure in their work lives and build a community of peers. Today the Grotto occupies an entire floor of an office building, with shared workspace for more than ninety published authors, journalists, fiction writers, filmmakers, and poets. In addition, the Grotto has introduced a Grotto Fellowship program to help inspire and nurture new writers, as well as Grotto Classes, a four-session-a-year educational program with writing classes taught by working writers. Visit sfgrotto.org for more information.